W9-BQJ-487

LASERS

FACTS ON FILE
SCIENCE SOURCEBOOKS

LASERS

THE NEW TECHNOLOGY OF LIGHT

CHARLENE W. BILLINGS

Facts On File
New York • Oxford

LASERS: THE NEW TECHNOLOGY OF LIGHT

Copyright © 1992 by Charlene W. Billings

All rights reserved. No part of this book may be reproduced or utilized in any form or by any means, electronic or mechanical, including photocopying, recording, or by any information storage or retrieval systems, without permission in writing from the publisher. For information contact:

Facts On File, Inc.
460 Park Avenue South
New York NY 10016
USA

Facts On File Limited
c/o Roundhouse Publishing Ltd.
P.O. Box 140
Oxford OX2 7SF
United Kingdom

Library of Congress Cataloging-in-Publication Data
Billings, Charlene W.
Lasers : the new technology of light / Charlene W. Billings.
p. cm. — (Facts On File science sourcebooks)
Includes bibliographical references and index.
Summary: Explains what lasers are and how they work and examines their various uses.
ISBN 0-8160-2630-0
1. Lasers—Juvenile literature. [1. Lasers.] I. Title. II. Series.
TA1682.B55 1992
621.36'6—dc20 92-7324

A British CIP catalogue record for this book is available from the British Library.

Facts On File books are available at special discounts when purchased in bulk quantities for businesses, associations, institutions or sales promotions. Please contact our Special Sales Department in New York at 212/683-2244 (dial 800/322- 8755 except in NY, AK or HI) or in Oxford at 865/728399.

Text design by Ron Monteleone
Jacket design by Amy Gonzalez
Composition by Ron Monteleone/Facts On File, Inc.
Manufactured by the Maple-Vail Book Manufacturing Group
Printed in the United States of America

10 9 8 7 6 5 4 3 2 1

This book is printed on acid-free paper.

OTHER BOOKS BY THE AUTHOR

Spring Peepers Are Calling

Salamanders

Scorpions

Microchip: Small Wonder

Space Station: Bold New Step Beyond Earth

Fiber Optics: Bright New Way to Communicate

Christa McAuliffe: Pioneer Space Teacher

Grace Hopper: Navy Admiral and Computer Pioneer

Loon: Voice of the Wilderness

Superconductivity: From Discovery to Breakthrough

Pesticides: Necessary Risk

To scientists everywhere whose vision and dedication have made possible the "splendid light" of lasers for the good of all

CONTENTS

Acnowledgments ix

Chapter 1. Harnessing Light 1
What Is a Laser? 2
How Does a Laser Work? 3

Chapter 2. The Nature of Light 6
The Stuff of Atoms 6
Particles or Waves? 8
The Electromagnetic Spectrum: A Range of Energy 9
Laser Light Is Organized 11

Chapter 3. From Maser to Laser 14
A Bright Idea 15
The "Optical Maser" 15
Lighting up a New Era 17

Chapter 4. An Explosion of Lasers 19
Solid Lasers 19
Gas Lasers 21
Liquid Lasers 25
Semiconductor Lasers 26
Switching on Powerful Pulses 27

Chapter 5. Communications: Listening to Light 29
The Photophone 29
Ali Javan and the Gas Laser 31

Chapter 6. Communications: Guiding Laser Light 34
How Optical Fibers Are Made 35
Sound and Data Transmission 36
Are Solitions a Solution? 39
Advantages of Fiber Optic Communications 40

Chapter 7. Lasers Are Revolutionizing Surgery 43
Laser Eye Surgery: Restoring the Gift of Sight 43
Other Kinds of Surgery 50

Chapter 8. Dentists Lighten Up 58
Painless Dentistry 58
New Teeth from Old 60

Chapter 9. Laser Recording 61
CDs and CDVs 61
Laser Libraries and an Information-Rich Society 65

Chapter 10. Lasers in Industry 68
Lightening the Work Load 68
Making Miniaturization Possible 72

Chapter 11. More Uses for Lasers 75
Measuring Distances and Motion 75
Lasers and Law Enforcement 81
Lasers in Construction and Agriculture 83
Laser Printers 84
Uniform Product Code 84
Shedding New Light on Old Art and History 85
Of Laser Light Shows and Fairies 87

Chapter 12. Lasers: Searchlight for Scientific Research 88
Chemical and Biological Research 88
Isotope Separation and Fission 89
Fusion: Recipe for a Star! 90
Laser Launches, Lightcraft, and Star Wars 93

Chapter 13. Holography 95
A New Dimension in Photography 95
Applications of Holography 98
Holographic Art 101

Chapter 14. Safety with Lasers 102

Conclusion 105
Appendix of Prefixes 106
Glossary 107
Further Reading 112
Index 114

ACKNOWLEDGMENTS

My sincere appreciation to all those who have helped to provide information and photographs for this book. Special thanks to my husband, Barry, for giving technical guidance and for bringing me many enlightening resource materials.

“A splendid light has dawned on me . . .”

—Albert Einstein

1 HARNESSING LIGHT

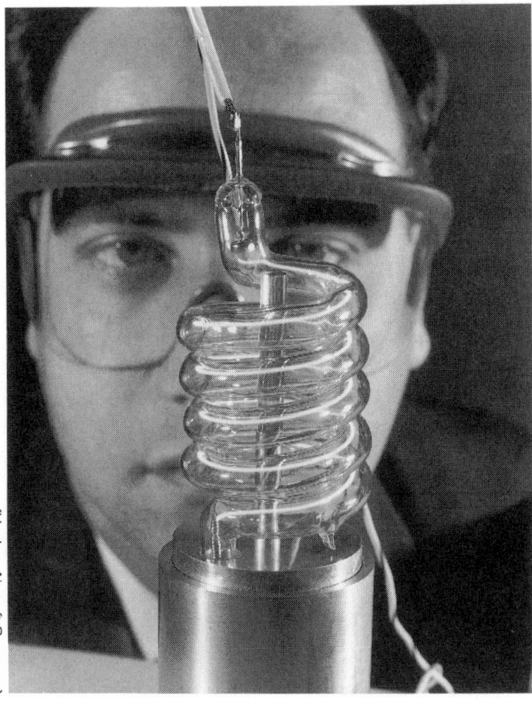

(Hughes Aircraft Company)

Dr. Theodore Maiman studies the laser's main parts, a light source surrounding a rod of synthetic ruby crystal through which excited atoms generate the intense beams.

On May 16, 1960, Dr. Theodore Maiman successfully operated the first laser in the laboratories of the Hughes Aircraft Company, in Malibu, California. A synthetic ruby rod less than one inch long and about one-third of an inch in diameter was placed inside a spiral-shaped, glass flashtube. The flat ends of the ruby rod had been carefully polished and coated with silver. A sudden burst of light was set off in the flashtube, and a brief, slim beam of red laser light brighter than the sun bolted from the end of the ruby rod. The energy of light had been harnessed. The laser was invented!

What Is a Laser?

The word *laser* is short for *l*ight *a*mplification by *s*timulated *e*mission of *r*adiation. Laser light is an entirely new kind of light, more brilliant, more intense than anything found in nature. Laser light can be so powerful that it can vaporize any known material on Earth in a fraction of a second. It can bore holes in the toughest metals or easily pierce the hardness of a diamond.

In contrast, less powerful, exquisitely precise beams from other kinds of lasers can be used to perform extremely delicate operations, such as surgery on the human eye. Laser light can be controlled very exactly and can be produced in a steady beam called a *continuous wave* or in rapid-fire, bursts of light called *pulses*.

Although the underlying principles of lasers had been known for over 40 years, the demonstration of the first laser opened the floodgates to one of the most exciting and far-reaching technological developments of the 20th century. Within a few years of the first laser demonstration, many different kinds of lasers were being used as practical tools in a variety of ways. And, as we shall see, lasers have brought about truly revolutionary new technologies that will continue to affect our lives in the future.

Today, a broad spectrum of lasers is being used all around us. Supermarkets and many other large-volume retail stores use lasers to automatically scan, record prices, and inventory items we buy at the checkout counter. Video systems use laser light to "read" video disks and produce a moving picture with an accompanying sound track. Large quantities of information are stored on laser disks to be read on a computer screen or printed onto paper as hard copy by a laser printer.

In medicine, laser light is used as a new kind of bloodless "scalpel" that seals blood vessels as it cuts through tissue during operations such as the removal of a diseased gall bladder. Lasers also are making some visits to the dentist less painful and are used to manufacture dental crowns and bridges.

Lasers are used in industry for heat treating of metals, welding parts together, and precisely aligning equipment. Lasers are used to measure exactly both very large and very small distances. In addition, lasers are teamed with optical fibers for better data transmission and improved telephone communication. Lasers are changing the ways scientists do research. And lasers also may create a new source of electric power similar to the process our sun uses to produce energy.

How Does a Laser Work?

Every laser has certain basic parts. First there must be an *energy source*. Often the energy source is electricity, but a strong source of ordinary light, a chemical reaction, or even another laser can also be used.

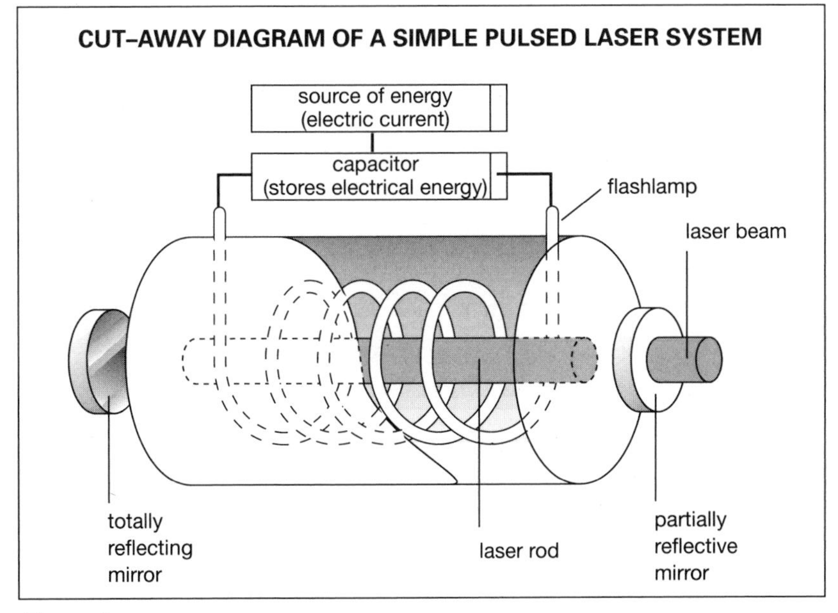

Figure 1

Another necessary component of a laser is known as the *active medium*. The active medium is a material that can absorb and release energy. It may be a solid, such as a ruby or other crystal, a liquid, such as certain dyes, or a gas, such as carbon dioxide. The laser beam is actually generated in the active medium.

The final basic part of a laser is the *feedback mechanism*. The feedback mechanism consists of two mirrors or other reflective surfaces placed at each end of the active medium. The mirrors build up the strength of the laser beam. One of the mirrors, known as the *output coupler*, is only partially reflective.

Laser action occurs in several steps. The energy source gives off a flash of light that is absorbed by the active medium. The absorbed energy excites some of the atoms of the active medium to a higher energy level. Repeated bursts of light from the energy source may continue to excite, or *pump,* the atoms of the active medium. When there are more excited, high-energy atoms than low-energy atoms present in the active medium, a *population inversion* exists. Population inversion is necessary for laser action to occur.

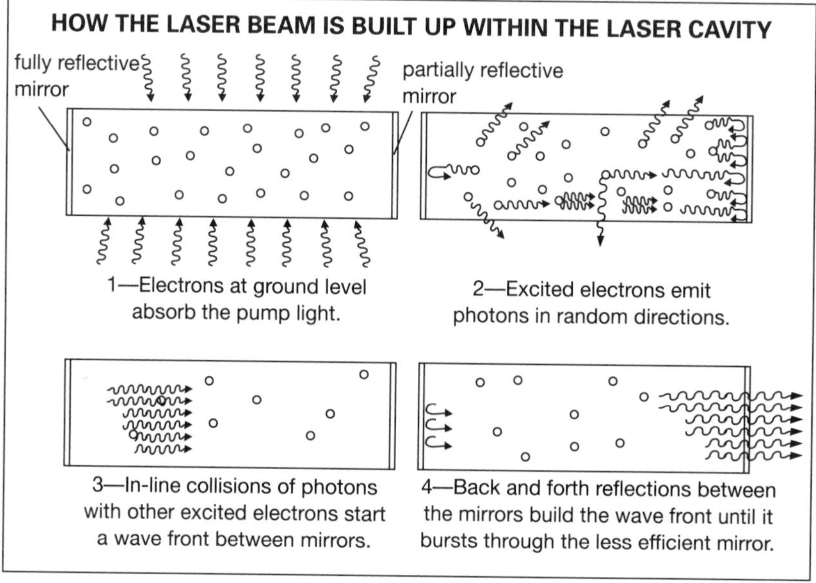

Figure 2

During laser action, high-energy atoms returning to a low-energy level get rid of their excess energy by giving out tiny amounts of light called *photons.* This light, in turn, excites other atoms in active medium to release light as well. In this way, a chain reaction of growing energy cascades through the active medium. More and more atoms in the active medium release tiny amounts of light. This phenomenon is known as *stimulated emission.*

The mirrors at the ends of the laser bounce emitted light back into the active medium, further intensifying the light, a process called *amplification.* As the light generated inside the laser grows more and more intense, it becomes powerful enough to escape through the partially silvered output coupler as laser light.

Lasers usually are named after the active medium. For instance, a solid piece of ruby is the active medium in a ruby laser. The rhodamine laser uses rhodamine, a fluorescent liquid dye, as the active medium. The carbon dioxide gas laser uses carbon dioxide as the active medium and the helium-neon gas laser uses a mixture of the gases helium and neon. In semi-conductor or diode lasers, crystals that are part of small electronic devices are the active medium.

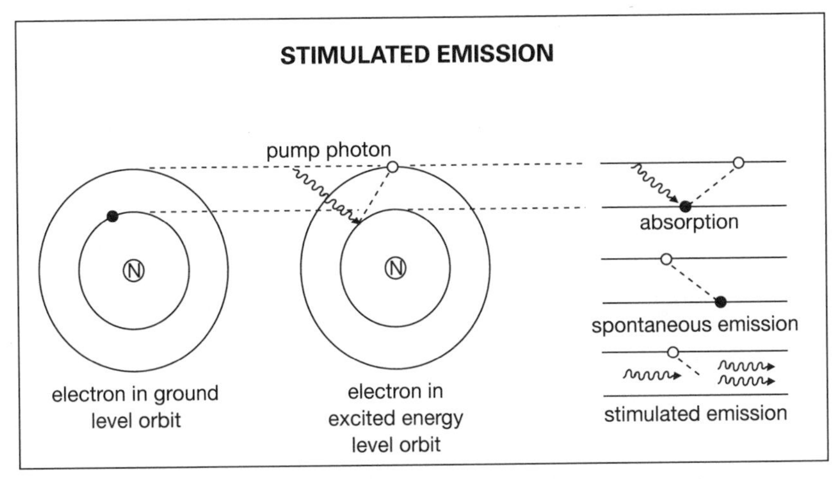

Figure 3: *A photon from the pump energy drives the ground-level electron to its excited orbit. It either returns to ground level by spontaneous emission or is stimulated to emit its excess energy by being struck by another photon. In stimulated emission, both photons emerge "in step."*

2 THE NATURE OF LIGHT

Some of the knowledge needed to build the first laser was known since the early part of the 20th century. However, before the first laser could be built, scientists needed to learn more about atomic structure and behavior.

The Stuff of Atoms

All matter is made up of particles called atoms. Atoms are the smallest unit of a chemical element that can exist and still be that element. Submicroscopic in size, millions of atoms can fit on the head of a pin.

In 1910 and 1911, Ernest Rutherford and two of his students carried out experiments in Cambridge, England, that showed that an atom is made up of smaller particles known as *protons*, *neutrons*, and *electrons*. At the center of the atom is the nucleus, which is made up of protons and neutrons (except for the element hydrogen, which has only one proton in its nucleus). Protons have a positive electrical charge, and neutrons have no electrical charge.

Revolving in orbits around the nucleus are electrons, which are negatively charged. The number of electrons in orbit around the nucleus of an atom is equal to the number of protons in the nucleus of the atom. Thus the negative charge of the electrons balances the positive charge of the protons so that an atom is normally neutral, or has no charge.

The first orbit, or energy level, nearest the nucleus may contain up to two electrons. Up to eight electrons may occupy the second orbit further away from the nucleus, 18 electrons the third orbit and so on, with a specific number of electrons possible for each energy level. The energy levels have historically been assigned letters to identify them.

The first band is the K band, and successive energy bands as they move further away from the nucleus are the L, M, N, O, P, and Q bands. Electrons in the outermost orbit from the nucleus have the highest energy level.

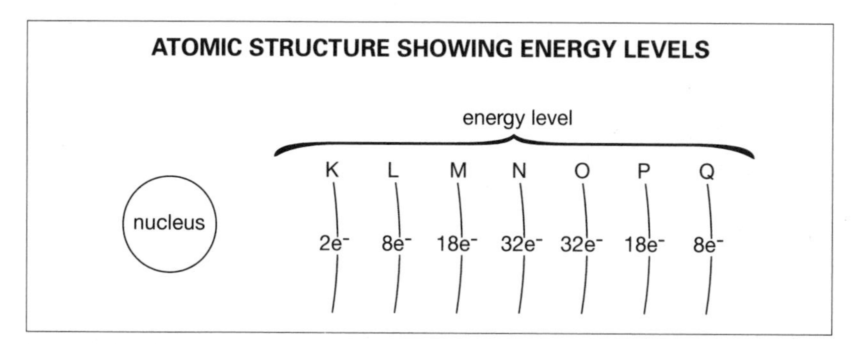

Figure 4: *Electron shells and the maximum number of electrons that may be present in each*

In 1913, Niels Bohr proposed a theory to explain the observed behavior of atoms. He imagined an atom as a miniature solar system, with the electrons spinning in one or more orbits around the central nucleus, much like the planets revolving around the sun. And although this view of atomic structure is now considered inadequate, it still is useful to explain atomic behavior.

According to the Bohr model of an atom, electrons revolve in specified orbits around the nucleus without emitting radiant energy. An atom is in its *ground state* when all of its electrons are at their lowest energy level. This is the normal, stable state of an atom.

However, Bohr also postulated that an electron may suddenly jump from one specified orbit in an atom to another. To move from a lower energy level to a higher energy level, an electron must gain energy. To move from a higher energy level to a lower energy level, an electron must lose energy. An electron can jump from one energy level to another by either absorbing or emitting radiant energy or light.

If energy from an outside source excites the electrons in orbit around the nucleus of an atom, one or more of the electrons may absorb enough energy to jump to the next higher orbit, or energy level. The atom is then in an excited, unstable state and can only remain in that state for a very brief time known as the *excited state lifetime.* When the electron drops back to a lower energy level, it gives out radiant energy in the form of light.

Particles or Waves?

In 1860 James Clerk Maxwell was able to prove experimentally that light travels in waves. He devised a set of equations to describe the wave nature of light and showed that the electromagnetic waves he theorized about traveled at precisely the speed of light. Maxwell also demonstrated that electromagnetic waves had other properties associated with light; they could be reflected, refracted, diffracted, and produce an interference pattern.

Nevertheless, scientists continued to be puzzled about some of the characteristics of light. They found that in some ways light behaved as though it consisted of streams of particles.

About the turn of the century, the physicist Max Planck theorized that light consisted of exact units or packets of radiant energy, which he called *quanta* (plural of *quantum,* the Latin word for how much). He further suggested that a single quantum of light could not be subdivided.

Some substances can absorb radiant energy and then later give it off as light. When this occurs naturally in an atom, it is called *spontaneous emission.* The visible light liberated in spontaneous emission is in the form of packets of light or quanta of energy. The electrons of an atom only can absorb or emit light of a particular frequency that "fits" one of their possible energy jumps.

Albert Einstein called the basic unit of light emitted during spontaneous emission a photon. He chose the name to emphasize that quanta of light behave like moving particles. The *phot-* syllable in the word *photon* is from the Greek word for light and the *-on* syllable is from the name of the particle in an atom that can move about, the electron.

In technical papers he wrote between 1905 and 1916, Einstein proposed that one photon could be absorbed entirely by a single electron. In addition, he theorized that a photon emitted by an atom could cause another excited like atom to emit a second photon. Einstein called this *stimulated emission.* So taken with his insight was Einstein that he joyfully told a friend, "A splendid light has dawned on me . . ."

If sufficient numbers of excited atoms are gathered in a small confined space, as in a laser, enough stimulated emission can occur to produce laser action.

Einstein and many other scientists explored the structure and behavior of atoms as well as the nature of light. Their work laid the foundation for the development of lasers.

(American Institute of Physics, Niels Bohr Library Photo Collection, Burndy Library)

Albert Einstein

The Electromagnetic Spectrum: A Range of Energy

The light human eyes can see is only a very narrow band of the radiant energy all around us that makes up the *electromagnetic spectrum.* This energy continuum is made up of radio waves, microwaves, infrared rays, visible light, ultraviolet light, X rays, and gamma rays. All of these kinds of energy consist of waves, or *oscillations,* that can cause or induce electrical and magnetic effects, hence the name *electromagnetic spectrum.*

The energy in this broad spectrum may be generated naturally by sources in the universe such as the sun and the stars or may be generated by oscillating electrons in metal antennas, as in the case of radio waves. Except for visible light, the forms of energy in the electromagnetic spectrum normally cannot be detected by our eyes.

The natural light humans can see is a form of energy that travels through the air in waves. The waves radiate outward from the light

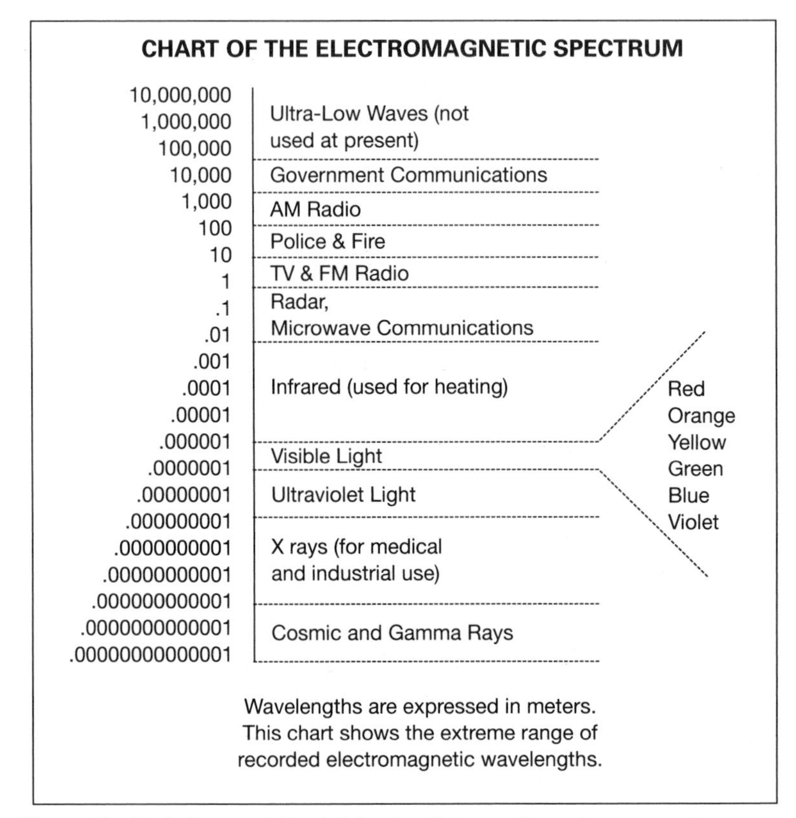

Figure 5: *Each figure at the left is the distance from the crest of one wave to the crest of the next. The portion of the electromagnetic spectrum visible to the human eye is only a narrow band of the total spectrum.*

source in all directions. Light waves have a shape like the waves that travel down a rope anchored at one end when you jiggle it up and down at the other end.

The distance between adjacent crests of waves traveling along the rope is a *wavelength*. The number of waves passing a given point along the rope in a specific amount of time is the *frequency*. For example, the frequency of radio waves is measured in units of cycles per second, and one cycle per second is equal to one Hertz.

The speed with which a wave moves along the rope is its *velocity*. An automobile's velocity is measured in the familiar units of miles or kilometers per hour. Nothing travels faster than light, with a velocity of 186,000 miles per second or 300,000 kilometers per second.

Using the rope again to visualize waves, you can make a lot of frequent, short waves by jiggling the rope up and down rapidly, or you can make a few less frequent, long waves by jiggling the rope up and down slowly. As the frequency of waves of energy in the electromagnetic spectrum gets higher, the wavelengths become shorter and the energy increases. As a visible example, the light waves our eyes see as the color blue are shorter and more frequent than the light waves our eyes see as the color red.

The electromagnetic waves with the lowest frequencies and the longest wavelengths are *radio waves*. Their frequencies may be as low as 10 per second and their wavelengths up to millions of meters long. Radio waves with wavelengths from a few tenths to about one thousandth of a meter are known as *microwaves*.

Infrared frequencies are intermediate between those of microwaves and red visible light. (The prefix *infra-* means below; the frequencies in infrared waves are below those of visible light.) The range of wavelengths for infrared is from about one micrometer (a micrometer, also known as a micron, is one millionth of a meter) to an indefinite upper wavelength sometimes set at 1,000 micrometers. The infrared portion of the electromagnetic spectrum sometimes is also called long-wave radiation. Although humans cannot see infrared frequencies, we sense this form of radiation as heat.

The next band of frequencies in the electromagnetic spectrum is *visible light*. Here, wavelengths are measured in mere *b*illionths of a meter. Though our eyes sense visible light as white light, it consists of a mixture of colors. As the wavelength is decreased, the color changes from red to orange to yellow to green to blue to violet. When ordinary visible light is passed through a prism, it is separated into the rainbow of colors known as the *visible spectrum*.

Just above visible light in the electromagnetic spectrum is *ultraviolet light* (UV) with frequencies that are higher than those of visible light. Frequencies higher than UV are *X rays* and still higher are *gamma rays*.

Laser Light Is Organized

Lasers produce a special light that is different from the white light that occurs in nature or from a source such as a flashlight or candle. Like the confusing mixture of interfering sounds we hear as noise, ordinary white light is a disorganized mixture of many different

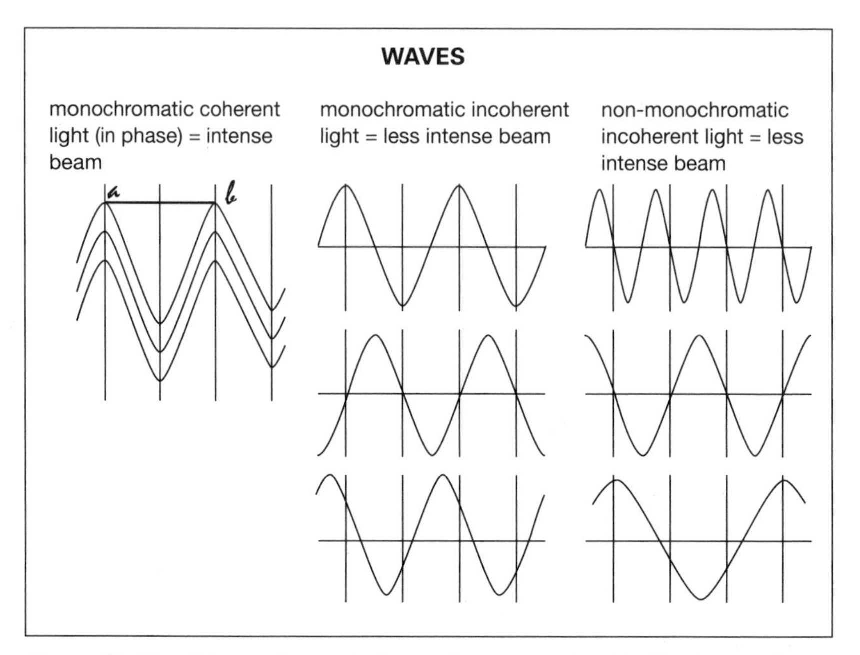

Figure 6: *The distance from a to b equals one wavelength. The beam of light is most intense when all of the waves are of the same wavelength or color and in phase with each other.*

wavelengths of light all jumbled together and traveling in different directions. For this reason it is called *incoherent* light.

Like a single, crystal clear musical tone, the light emitted from a laser is *all the same wavelength,* sometimes referred to as "pure" light. In addition, the light waves from a laser are synchronized to travel in step, or *in phase,* with each other. The crest of each wave is matched with the crest of all the other waves. For these reasons, laser light is highly organized and is called *coherent* light.

Another feature is that laser light is *directional.* It travels in straight beams that do not spread out as much as ordinary light does. For example, light beamed from a flashlight onto a wall 1,000 feet away would illuminate a circle about a 200 feet in diameter. However, light from a laser beamed over the same distance at the same wall would cover only about a one foot circle with light.

Because the light emitted by a laser is all of the same wavelength or frequency, it is all one color, or *monochromatic.* Ordinary light passed through a prism separates and spreads into the rainbow of assorted colors of the visible spectrum. However, laser light passed through a

(NASA)

In this 1968 photo, engineers at Goddard Space Flight Center are shown operating the continuous argon laser in an experiment to send a message by laser to a satellite in orbit, the Explorer XXXVI. *The photo depicts the straight, narrow characteristics of a laser beam.*

prism emerges from the prism as the same single, straight beam of color that entered.

3 FROM MASER TO LASER

(Columbia University, Office of Public Education)

A 1955 photo of Dr. Charles H. Townes and an associate, James P. Gordon, then a doctoral candidate at Columbia University, with the first maser. It was constructed by Townes, then a physics professor at Columbia, and his colleagues in work begun in 1952.

One morning in the spring of 1951, Dr. Charles H. Townes, a physicist from Columbia University, in New York City, was sitting on a park bench in Washington, D.C., waiting to go to a meeting of the American Physical Society. He had been asked by the U.S. Navy to try to find ways to extend the range of microwave frequencies that could be used in communications. The devices that already existed could not be made small enough to accommodate the high-frequency characteristics of microwaves.

A Bright Idea

While he was admiring the azalea blossoms, Townes was struck by the idea that molecules had the right characteristics to accomplish his aim. He wondered if the molecules of a gas could be stimulated by radiant energy of a specific wavelength to emit oscillations of the same frequency. Thus far no one had done such a thing.

Townes imagined a beam of heated gas molecules some of which would be in a high-energy state and some in a low-energy state. The molecules in the beam would be separated so that mostly high-energy molecules would enter a special resonating cavity. There, the excited molecules would be stimulated by a signal of a specific frequency to emit microwaves. If the walls of the resonating cavity were highly reflective, each time the molecules passed back and forth within the cavity a cascade of more and more microwaves would be emitted.

Townes's proposal was presented in May of 1951, at a conference at the University of Illinois. In addition, on December 31, 1951, the idea was outlined in the *Progress Report* of the Columbia Radiation Laboratory.

Back at Columbia University, Townes discussed his ideas with two colleagues, postdoctoral fellow Dr. Herbert Zeiger and graduate student James P. Gordon. The three set to work and by 1953 they had built a device that used ammonia gas as an active medium. Their invention was a source of high-frequency microwaves and was named a *maser,* which stands for *m*icrowave *a*mplification by *s*timulated *e*mission of *r*adiation.

About the same time, other physicists were attempting to devise a maser as well. Joseph Weber of the University of Maryland presented a paper entitled "The Possibility of Amplification of Microwaves by Systems Not in Equilibrium" in 1952 and published his article in June 1953. Others who were working on masers were Aleksander M. Prokhorov and Nikolai Basov of the Lebedev Physics Institute in Moscow.

In 1964, Townes, Prokhorov, and Basov all were recognized for their contribution when they shared the Nobel Prize for their work. The maser was the first practical application of Einstein's principles of stimulated emission.

The "Optical Maser"

Though masers proliferated rapidly in the 1950s, Townes and his brother-in-law, Dr. Arthur Schawlow of Bell Laboratories at Murray

(Stanford News Service)

In 1963, Dr. Arthur Schawlow demonstrated the selectivity of a laser in action. He aimed its beam at two balloons, a blue balloon inflated inside a clear one. The energy of the laser's beam was not absorbed by the clear balloon and passed harmlessly through it. But the blue balloon absorbed the energy of the laser beam and burst.

Hill, New Jersey, were already thinking about ways to generate wavelengths shorter than microwaves.

The two men collaborated on a paper that they published in the December 1958 issue of *Physical Review*, entitled "Infrared and Optical Masers." The paper described important differences between the requirements necessary to build a maser that would emit microwaves and the requirements to build an "optical maser" that would emit visible light. Before their paper was published, they also applied for U.S. patent number 2,929,922.

Meanwhile a graduate student at Columbia University, Gordon Gould, also was working on proposals for stimulated emission in the wavelength range of visible light. Because Gould did not apply for a patent until after Schawlow and Townes had done so, he did not receive the same recognition as Schawlow and Townes.

However, in the course of his work, Gordon Gould referred to the optical maser in his notebooks by the name *laser*, and so he is credited with coining the word that we still use today. As already mentioned, laser stands for *l*ight *a*mplification by *s*timulated *e*mission of *r*adiation. In 1977 and again in 1979, separate patents for laser concepts that Gould described in his notebooks were issued to him.

The optical maser that Schawlow and Townes proposed in their 1958 paper used sodium or potassium metallic vapors. The electrons in these vapors could be excited, or "pumped," by an outside energy source to high energy levels and then stimulated to emit visible light.

The paper also is important because it suggested a method that would solve the difficult problem of how to design a resonant cavity for visible light wavelengths that were 10,000 times smaller than microwaves.

Schawlow and Townes's idea was to contain the active medium in a cylinder with transparent sides and reflecting mirrors at both ends. During emission, photons that were not traveling parallel to the main axis of the cylinder would leave the tube through the transparent walls. On the other hand, photons traveling parallel to the axis of the cylinder would be reflected by the mirrors at each end of the cylinder. As these photons bounced back and forth through the active medium, the number of synchronized photons of the same frequency would multiply with each sweep through the active medium.

In order for the laser beam to finally escape from the cylinder, Schawlow and Townes proposed that one of the reflecting mirrors at the ends of the cylinder be only partially reflecting. In this way, some of the light generated by their optical maser would be able to escape the device.

In 1959, Schawlow published a suggestion that it should be possible to build a light-maser using a solid active medium and he mentioned using a ruby crystal for this purpose.

Lighting up a New Era

Another researcher, Dr. Theodore H. Maiman, had been working on the idea of a solid optical maser using a synthetic ruby. On May 16, 1960, Maiman observed the historic first laser action at the Hughes Research Laboratories using a ruby crystal as the active medium. Later, the original ruby crystal, which Maiman still keeps in his possession, was replaced with one of better optical quality.

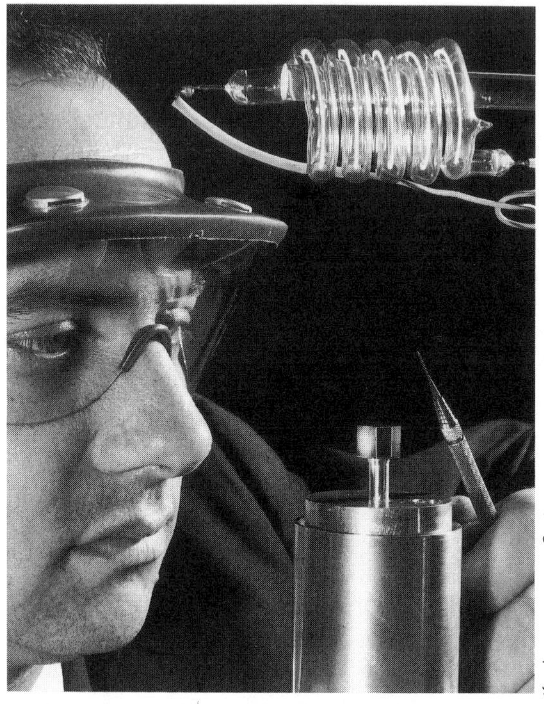

Dr. Theodore Maiman is shown with a cube of synthetic ruby crystal that forms the heart of a laser. The light source (at top) is used to excite the tightly packed atoms in the ruby, which amplify the laser's light into an intense parallel beam.

(Hughes Aircraft Company)

The electrons of atoms in the synthetic ruby crystal were stimulated or "pumped," to a higher energy level than normal by flashes of intense light from a xenon flashtube, similar to the kind used by photographers. Photons emitted by the excited atoms were amplified countlessly as they bounced back and forth between the mirrored ends of the ruby rod. A dazzling, powerful 10,000 watt pulse of red laser light burst forth from one end of the ruby rod.

4 AN EXPLOSION OF LASERS

(Hughes Aircraft Company)

This photo shows a ruby laser cutting through a sheet of extremely hard tantalum metal in less than 1,000th of a second. The beam is a million times brighter than the sun.

With Dr. Maiman's success, an explosive new era of laser technology began. The ruby laser was the first in a proliferation of new lasers. Inspired, intrepid researchers rushed to learn if other kinds of materials could produce laser light.

Solid Lasers

Certain characteristics are necessary for a solid crystal to be useful in the laser process. The crystal must be transparent so that light can enter it to excite the active medium and so that the laser beam itself can escape. In addition, the atoms of the active medium must be capable of producing the desired wavelengths.

Crystals used for making lasers usually contain a small amount of an impurity not found in a pure crystal. The pure crystal is called the *host* material, and the process of adding an impurity is called *doping*. In the ruby laser crystal, aluminum oxide is the host material and chromium oxide is the doping material or impurity.

Besides ruby, crystals such as sapphire and garnet can be used to make solid lasers. Other examples of useful host crystals are combinations of tungsten and oxygen or molybdenum and oxygen. These may be doped with barium, strontium, calcium, or chromium to make laser crystals. In addition, high purity glass may be doped with neodymium.

Laser crystals are manufactured by combining powdered host material and powdered doping material. The two powders are mixed together and melted at very high temperatures (500° C to 1,700° C) in a heat-resistant bowl called a *crucible*.

A small seed crystal of the host material is attached to the end of a rod that is rotated like a high-speed drill. The seed crystal is lowered into the hot melted material. As the rod rotates, layer upon layer of the molten material solidifies onto the seed crystal. The heat of the melt and speed of rotation of the rod are carefully controlled. As the crystal forms, the rotating rod is gradually withdrawn from the melt to achieve a uniform diameter.

The crystal growing process produces a *boule*. The boule is cooled, annealed, or heat treated, cut to proper shape, and polished. Depending upon the materials used, the resultant laser crystal may be only about the size of a fountain pen or up to several feet long.

Before the end of 1960, another type of solid laser had been devised. Peter P. Sorokin and M. J. Stevenson at International Business Machines Corporation (IBM) built a laser using calcium fluoride doped with uranium. In 1961, L. F. Johnson and K. Nassau demonstrated a neodymium laser. It used calcium tungstate as the host material and neodymium as a dopant. The first neodymium-glass laser was demonstrated by Elias Snitzer at American Optical, also in 1961.

Three years later, J. E. Geusic, H. M. Marcos, and L. G. Van Uitert demonstrated a solid laser that now has many commerical applications. It is the yttrium aluminum garnet, or YAG, laser. The YAG laser is doped with neodymium.

Solid lasers are not very efficient. The energy transitions that take place in a solid laser generate heat. In order to allow solid lasers time to cool, they are usually operated as pulsed lasers rather than as lasers that produce a continuous beam of light. On the other hand, solid lasers can produce extremely powerful pulses of laser light. The largest neodymium lasers, for example, can provide as much as 25 trillion watts of power in a single pulse. (One horsepower is equivalent to 746 watts, so 25 trillion watts is about 33,512,100,000 horsepower.)

Gas Lasers

A gas laser circulates a certain type of gas within a sealed transparent chamber that may look like a neon sign or the tube of a fluorescent lamp. As the gas circulates, it passes over two electrodes, one positively charged and the other negatively charged. Electrons streaming between the electrodes pump the electrons in the atoms of the circulating gas to high energy levels.

Unlike a solid, a gas can flow or move. As the gas circulates within the tube, the excited atoms drop to a lower energy level as they move away from the electrodes. When the electrons of the excited gas atoms drop back to a lower energy level, they emit photons. These are reflected back and forth between mirrors to amplify the effect, just as in the solid ruby laser. When a usable level of laser light is achieved, the beam passes out through a partially transparent output mirror. The helium-neon gas laser now is one of the most common gas lasers. As the name suggests, the active medium consists of a mixture of about 10 parts helium gas to one part neon gas. In a helium-neon gas laser, the laser beam is generated by the neon atoms.

Early attempts to make neon lasers ran into difficulties because researchers had trouble finding a way to pump the neon atoms to an excited state. The problems were solved by scientists at Bell Telephone Research Group by adding helium gas and then exciting it with a small radio transmitter. This laser emitted wavelengths in the invisible, near infrared region of the electromagnetic spectrum.

Other scientists later discovered that the helium-neon laser could emit another wavelength of 632.8 nanometers (a nanometer is a billionth of a meter) that produced a visible red light. This red wavelength has become the standard for helium-neon lasers.

Unlike the solid ruby laser that produces pulses of light, the helium-neon laser can produce a continuous laser beam or pulses of radiation. And although the power output of a helium-neon laser is usually measured in thousandths of a watt (much lower than that of a ruby laser), the continuous beam that is emitted is almost perfectly coher-

(American Institute of Physics, Niels Bohr Library Photo Collection)

Ali Javan with N. G. Basov, another scientist, at a 1959 conference on quantum electronics

ent. Because a helium-neon gas laser can be controlled very precisely, it is especially useful for communications.

Helium-neon gas lasers are safe enough to be used in schools and laboratories for experiments. Other uses are in the construction industry and for artistic displays. Helium-neon lasers are small in size and not as expensive as other types of lasers.

One of the most versatile lasers available today is the carbon dioxide gas laser. There are several types of carbon dioxide gas lasers, but the active medium in all of them is usually a mixture of carbon dioxide, nitrogen, and another gas, often helium.

Generally, the amount of carbon dioxide and nitrogen gases in a carbon dioxide laser are about the same, but the predominant gas present is helium. Approximately 10 percent of the gas mixture is carbon dioxide, 10 percent is nitrogen, and the remaining 80 percent helium.

Each of the three gases present in a carbon dioxide gas laser serves a distinct purpose, but it is the carbon dioxide that emits the laser light. The nitrogen gas absorbs energy and then helps to excite the carbon dioxide molecules by transferring its energy to the carbon dioxide molecules during collisions. The helium gas aids in heat transfers. It also helps the carbon dioxide molecules return to their normal, or ground-state, energy levels.

Carbon dioxide gas lasers are efficient when compared to some other types of lasers. A carbon dioxide gas laser can operate continuously if the gas mixture is kept moving through the laser tube and cooled in a heat exchanger. Large carbon dioxide gas lasers also can produce pulses of laser light measured in billions of watts of power. Their extraordinary power output is capable of vaporizing any known material so that it disappears into thin air.

Other types of carbon dioxide lasers have different structures. For example, in some carbon dioxide gas lasers, the flow of gas is at right angles to the axis of the laser tube. The gas flows into and out of the laser cavity at a much faster rate than if it were streaming from one end of the tube to the other. This arrangement allows excess heat to be removed quickly. These *transverse flow* carbon dioxide lasers are used commercially and can produce laser power in the order of 15 kilowatts (a kilowatt is 1,000 watts).

Transverse excitation atmospheric, or *TEA, lasers* operate near atmospheric pressure. As their name also suggests, they are structured much like a transverse carbon dioxide laser. The electric voltage used to excite the gas in a TEA laser is applied along the length of the laser tube. TEA lasers range in size from tabletop models to large lasers the size of a dumpster. TEA lasers produce intense, short pulses of microsecond duration.

In *waveguide* carbon dioxide lasers, the inside diameter of the carbon dioxide laser tube is only about two millimeters. Waveguide carbon dioxide lasers can produce continuous wave laser beams of from under one watt to about 50 watts in power. They can be tuned to produce discrete wavelengths that are emitted by the energy levels available in carbon dioxide gas molecules. Great advantages to these carbon dioxide lasers are their small size and low cost.

Some carbon dioxide gas lasers are known as *gas-dynamic lasers.* In these, carbon dioxide molecules are excited to high energy levels when the hot gas is rapidly expanded into a cool near-vacuum after being under high pressure.

Some lasers are stimulated by chemical reactions instead of an outside source of energy. *Chemical lasers* most often utilize gases as the active medium and are similar to the gas-dynamic laser in design. In certain chemical reactions, the end products of the reaction are in excited energy states that are capable of emitting photons. Some chemical lasers have produced pulses of energy as enormous as 200 gigawatts. A gigawatt is 1 billion watts of power.

Some gas lasers are labeled *ion lasers.* The term is used to refer to lasers that use ionized rare gases as the active medium. The most commonly used gases for these lasers are argon and krypton. Ionized neon and xenon have also been demonstrated to produce laser action, but they are not used as often.

When an atom is excited sufficiently to remove completely one (or more) of its electrons, it is *ionized.* The atom now becomes a positive *ion* because there are more positively charged protons in the nucleus than negatively charged electrons in orbit around the nucleus. (Atoms that gain electrons and so have a negative charge are also known as ions.)

The gases in ion lasers are excited by an electric discharge. Because the ionized gases are extremely hot and the electric current is very high, the material forming the laser tube and the electrodes providing the current can deteriorate rapidly. For these reasons, the design of ion lasers is faced with several difficulties that limit their efficiency and use.

Both argon and krypton gas lasers can produce *continuous-wave* (CW) laser light with a power range of from a few milliwatts to 10 or 20 watts. Argon gas lasers can emit ultraviolet and infrared radiation as well as blue, green, yellow, red, or even white light. Krypton lasers

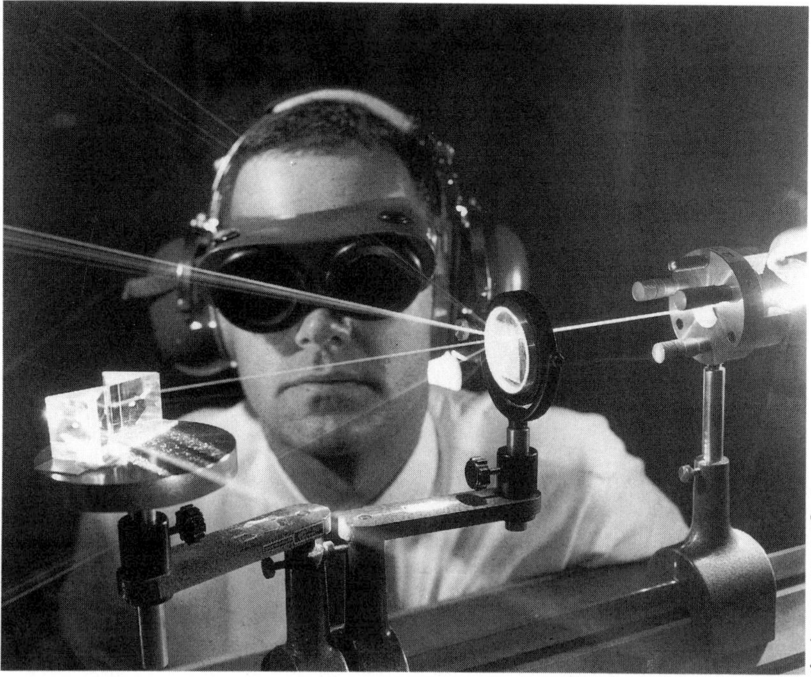

(Hughes Aircraft Company)

This continuous wave argon ion laser, which has power up to eight watts at different wavelengths, or colors, in the blue-green region of the visible spectrum, is operated by Dr. A. Stevens Halsted.

have a weaker output power than argon lasers but are useful because they also emit a wide range of visible wavelengths of light.

An *excimer laser* belongs to a family of gas lasers that produce nanosecond-long, powerful pulses at wavelengths near or in the ultraviolet portion of the electromagnetic spectrum. These lasers use mixtures of gases. The bulk of the gas mixture is a gas such as helium or neon that aids in energy transfer. A rare gas is the source of the laser action and usually makes up only one-half to 12 percent of the total mixture. The important excimer laser gases are krypton fluoride, xenon fluoride, argon fluoride, and xenon chloride. An excimer laser can generate pulses of over 1 billion watts of power.

Liquid Lasers

Lasers that use liquids as the active medium have the advantages of being more concentrated than a gas and of being able to be circulated and cooled. In 1966, Peter P. Sorokin and J. R. Lankard at IBM Corporation's Watson Research Center in Yorktown Heights, New York, demonstrated the first *liquid dye laser.* Since then hundreds of fluorescent dyes have been found to produce laser action. Dyes can emit laser beams with a wide range of wavelengths and thus have the great advantage of being *tunable.* The user can select from a range of available fine-tuned wavelengths the one most suited to his or her purpose. Liquid dye lasers can emit laser beams from about 250 nanometers in the ultraviolet through the whole visible spectrum to 1,800 nanometers in the infrared.

In a liquid dye laser, the dye is the active medium. It is usually dissolved in a liquid solvent such as alcohol or ethylene glycol (antifreeze). The source of energy for a liquid dye laser is usually a flashlamp or another laser. An example of a liquid dye laser is the rhodamine 6G laser. The active medium, the dye rhodamine 6G, fluoresces when light strikes it. An argon or a krypton ion laser may be the energy source.

The emitted light from the rhodamine 6G laser can be a broad range of frequencies from 570 to 655 nanometers and includes the orange color light of 590 nanometers that the dye fluoresces naturally. Dye lasers such as the rhodamine 6G laser are tunable using optical lenses and prisms to select the desired wavelength.

Liquid dye lasers are capable of emitting ultrashort pulses of laser light measured in *femtoseconds* (a quadrillionth of a second). These make possible the investigation of rapid processes in nature, such as chemical reactions, by effectively freezing the motion of the molecules on film. Liquid dye lasers also are used in *spectroscopy,* a method used to investigate the physical processes and energy levels within atoms and molecules.

Semiconductor Lasers

Lasers that are as small as a grain of salt can be made with semiconductor materials. Some materials such as copper, aluminum, gold, and other metals easily allow electricity to pass through them. They are called *conductors.* Other materials such as plastic, glass, and rubber do not allow electricity to pass through them. These are *insulators.* A *semiconductor* is neither a good insulator nor a good conductor of electricity. Its properties lie somewhere in between. For

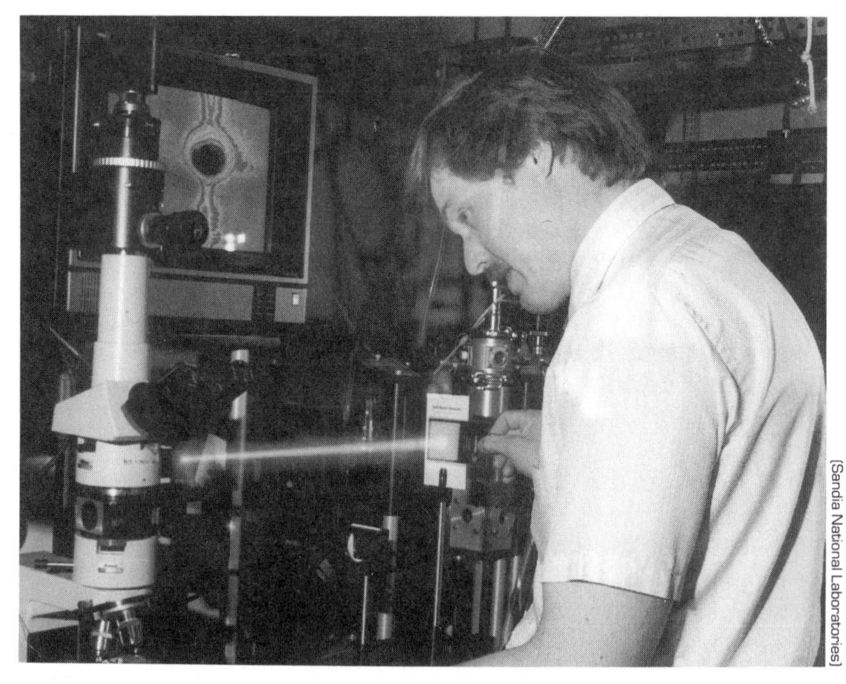

(Sandia National Laboratories)

Paul Gorley demonstrates the epitaxial surface-emitting semiconductor laser that he and his colleagues developed at Sandia National Laboratories. The laser structure is microscopic in size and emits from its surface, unlike conventional semiconductor lasers. It operates at room temperature with a continuous wave beam that is highly efficient.

this reason, under certain conditions, a semiconductor can serve as either an insulator or a conductor.

A semiconductor laser, also called a diode laser, uses electricity as the source of energy. Its structure is very different from other solid lasers but much like another kind of semiconductor known as a light-emitting diode, or LED. In a semiconductor laser, two kinds of semiconductor materials with different properties are joined together to form a junction. One material is doped with negatively charged atoms and is called the *n-type.* The other material is doped with positively charged atoms and is called the *p-type.*

Two of the surfaces of the semiconductor laser crystal are cut so smoothly that they are reflective. Coatings also may increase reflectivity. When an electric current is applied to a semiconductor laser, excited electrons move across the junction from the n-type to the p-type material and photons are emitted. Unlike an LED, the photons in a semiconductor laser are reflected back into the semiconductor material from the mirrorlike ends. Laser action occurs only when a sufficiently strong electrical current pumps the semiconductor laser.

One common type of semiconductor laser is made of gallium aluminum arsenide (GaAlAs). It emits tunable laser light at wavelengths between 750 and 900 nanometers and with power measured in milliwatts (a milliwatt is one one-thousandth of a watt). The emitted light may be either pulsed or continuous wave. Sometimes many semiconductor lasers are linked together with their output beams in phase. A *phased coupled array* can produce up to a watt of output power.

Switching on Powerful Pulses

Some lasers that have been described, such as liquid dye lasers and the argon ion laser, emit laser light in a continuous beam. Others, such as the ruby laser or a neodymium glass laser, produce laser light in pulses. Most of the pulsed lasers cannot operate as continuous wave lasers. Continuous wave lasers, on the other hand, can operate to produce short pulses of laser light that are more powerful than the energy normally available from such a laser.

A special switch called a *Pockels cell* can be used as a very fast shutter inside a continous wave laser. The shutter blocks the optical path between one mirror and the active medium. The active medium is strongly excited, but the shutter prevents laser action. When the shutter suddenly is opened, all of the built-up laser energy is released in one, brief enormous pulse. The power released in such a pulse is measured in megawatts and lasts from one to 30 nanoseconds.

Some applications require even shorter pulses of laser light. A technique called *mode-locking* uses a dye solution as a shutter. The dye absorbs photons being emitted by the active medium until it becomes *saturated,* or cannot absorb any more photons. Now photons produced by the active medium can pass through the dye unobstructed and laser action occurs.

Within a time frame as short as a few *picoseconds* (a picosecond is one one-trillionth of a second), the excited molecules in the dye return to their ground state energy level. Once back at ground state, the dye molecules again begin absorbing photons, effectively acting as a closed shutter once more.

5 COMMUNICATIONS: LISTENING TO LIGHT

[AT&T Archives]

Alexander Graham Bell's photophone

In 1880, Alexander Graham Bell tested an idea he had for a new way to communicate. The telephone he invented four years earlier used pulses of electricity carried through copper wires to transmit the human voice over long distances. His new device used a beam of sunlight traveling through air to transmit sound from one location to another.

The Photophone

The photophone consisted of several parts. At the sending end, the sound waves generated by a person's voice caused a mirror to vibrate. A beam of sunlight reflected off the mirror vibrated in the same way.

Another mirror at the receiving end of the photophone reflected the vibrating light beam onto a light-sensitive material, selenium. The selenium converted the light vibrations into electrical pulses that vibrated a speaker, just as in a regular telephone, to reproduce the sound of the person's voice.

The problems with the photophone were that it could not be used during nighttime and it was weather dependent. Rain, snow, dust, or fog blocked the vibrating light beam and made transmission impossible. Nevertheless, Alexander Graham Bell thought the photophone was one of his best ideas and believed that one day people would use beams of light to communicate over long distances.

Both light and electricity travel as vibrations or waves. However, light waves have very short wavelengths and much higher frequencies than electrical waves do. The higher the frequency, the more room there is to carry information. For this reason, much more information can be transmitted per second using light waves than can be sent by electricity traveling through copper wires.

As another comparison, electromagnetic waves carry information through the air in radio and television broadcasts. Standard A.M. radio broadcasts are at a frequency of a few thousand Hertz while F.M. radio is transmitted at a frequency of several million Hertz. In contrast, the frequency of light is about 100 million times greater than the radio waves of an F.M. broadcast.

Not until the 1960s and 1970s did long-distance communication via a beam of light become possible. With the invention of the laser, a source of brilliant, coherent light became available that was capable of sending signals to the moon, the distant planets, and even further into space. Also during this time period, optical fibers were being perfected that were capable of carrying laser light over long distances here on Earth without distortion or loss of brightness.

Laser communication through atmosphereless outer space is very efficient. For example, the National Aeronautics and Space Administration (NASA) developed an argon gas laser that could beam signals to an orbiting satellite equipped with a laser beam detector, *Explorer XXXVI,* launched in January, 1968. The laser, located at the Goddard Space Flight Center in Greenbelt, Maryland, sent information via laser light beams through space to the satellite detector. The message received in the form of laser beams then was converted to radio frequencies and broadcast back to Earth.

The U.S. Air Force developed a laser communication link with a satellite capable of handling data at a rate as high as one billion bits of information per second. It has the advantages of being nearly impossible to jam and provides complete security for transmission of important or secret information. Data can be transmitted between satellites, from ground to satellite, from satellite to ground, or from ship to ship.

Ali Javan and the Gas Laser

In order to make use of laser light for earthbound communications, a continuous beam was necessary rather than a pulsed beam. Bell scientist Ali Javan had envisioned a continuous laser beam that would use a mixture of two gases.

Manfred Brotherton describes the development of the gas laser in the Bell publication, *Laser: Challenge to Communications Science:*

> *On a December afternoon in 1960 at Bell Laboratories in Murray Hill, New Jersey, three scientists had been experimenting in a darkened room with a long glass tube that glowed like a neon sign. The forty-inch tube was connected to an assortment of mirrors,*

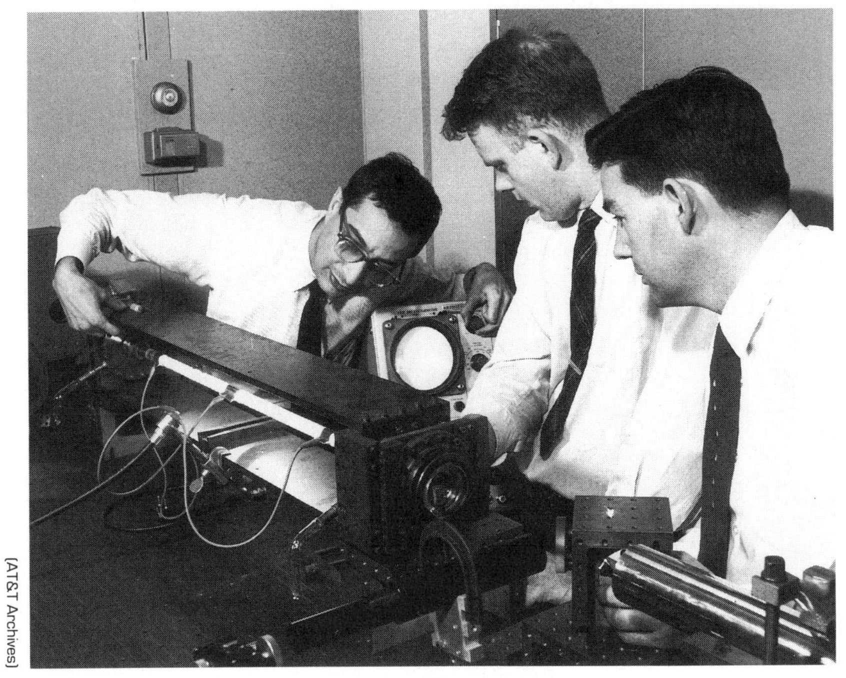

[AT&T Archives]

This 1961 photo shows Ali Javan, William Bennett, Jr., and Donald Herriott working on the helium-neon laser.

lenses, and electronic equipment that would have appeared strange indeed to an uninformed passerby."

Bell scientist Ali Javan had had an idea of how it might be possible to generate a continuous laser beam. Brotherton continues, "Tucked away in the storehouse of data was a fact about certain gases that caught Javan's imagination."

Javan knew that when certain pairs of gases are mixed and the atoms of one of the gases are excited to a higher energy level, their higher energy becomes trapped. However, when atoms of the high energy gas collide with the second gas in the mixture, their energy is transferred to the second gas. The second gas then releases the energy as light radiation. Javan pictured mirrored resonators at the end of the gas laser tube that would reflect the photons being released back and forth until enough energy was gained to produce a continuous laser beam.

Donald Herriott and William Bennett, Jr., tried to set up just such a laser at the Bell Laboratories using helium and neon gases. They excited the helium gas with a small radio transmitter. Whenever an excited helium atom collided with a neon atom in the ground state, all of its energy was transferred to the neon atom.

(Hughes Aircraft Company)

Dr. A. Stevens Halsted works with a continuous-wave argon ion laser.

However, when Herriott and Bennett tried to generate a continuous laser beam, the resonating mirrors shattered time after time. Quite by chance, Donald Herriott discovered that the problem could be solved by making an adjustment in the resonating mirrors. The researchers had persisted and won. A continuous laser beam was generated successfully.

In subsequent demonstrations, the Bell Laboratory researchers noted that the vibrations of the sound of their voices produced a corresponding vibration in the laser's output beam. Much to their surprise, when they attached an earphone to the oscilloscope that monitored the laser beam, they heard their own voices!

That day Ali Javan, who was away in New York, called the Bell Laboratories. Herriott and Bennett held the earphone they had been using near the mouthpiece of the telephone and shouted at the laser mirror to talk to Javan. They repeated the historic first words spoken over the telephone on March 10, 1876, by Alexander Graham Bell to his assistant, "Watson, come here. I want you!"

The helium-neon gas laser was announced by Javan, Bennett, and Herriott in February 1961.

6 COMMUNICATIONS: GUIDING LASER LIGHT

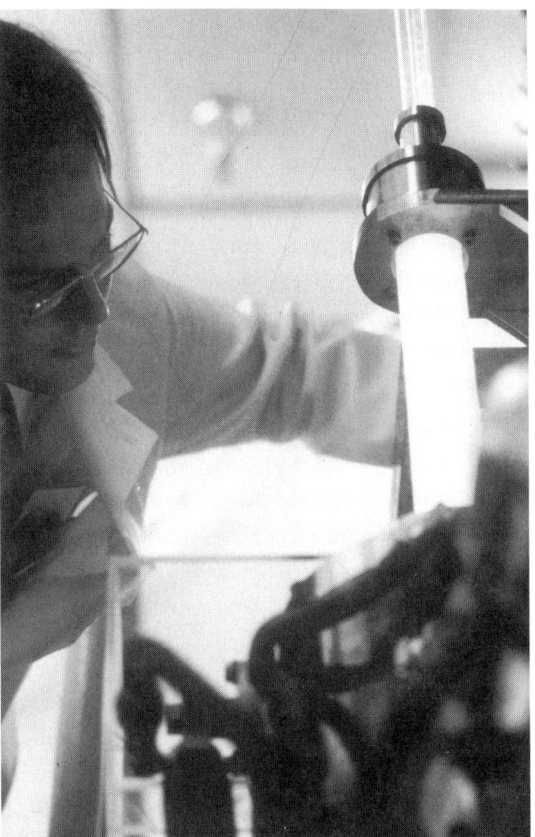

A glass preform is lowered into a draw tower to manufacture hair-thin optical fibers.

(Corning, Inc.)

The revolution in ground-based communications has depended, not only on the invention of the laser but also on the development of the *optical fiber*. An optical fiber is a hair-thin, flexible thread of ultra clear glass one-tenth of a millimeter in diameter. Optical fibers also are known as *lightguides* because they serve as pipelines or conduits for laser light.

How Optical Fibers Are Made

A glass optical fiber is made from silicon, the same material that is used to make microchips. Silicon is the main ingredient in sand, so it is very plentiful. An optical fiber has a glass inner *core* with an outer layer called the *cladding*.

The cladding is composed of a slightly different glass from the core. It acts like a mirror, totally reflecting the light beam traveling through the optical fiber back into the core of the fiber. The trapped light beam cannot escape from the optical fiber until it comes to the other end. For this reason, laser light traveling through an optical fiber does not lose its brightness.

Optical fibers have many advantages over copper wires for voice, information, or data transmission. Much more information can be sent by laser beam over a single optical fiber than by electricity over one copper wire. A single optical fiber can carry the same amount of information as a telephone cable containing 256 pairs of wires. A spool of optical fiber weighing only four and one-half pounds is capable of transmitting the same number of messages as 200 reels of copper wire weighing over eight tons!

Optical fibers are made in special clean rooms where the air is filtered to remove the smallest particles of dirt. The manufacturing process is known as modified chemical vapor deposition (MCVD). A hollow glass tube is mounted on a machine that rotates it along its long axis. A torch moves back and forth along the tube heating it to 1,600° C.

At the same time, a special gas is fed into the tube. The gas deposits a thin layer on the inside wall of the tube. Different gases are fed into the tube to add desired layers of different kinds of glass. When the process is complete, the gas is removed from the tube. The heat from the flaming torch is increased to 2,000° C. and the hollow tube collapses to form a solid glass rod known as a *preform*.

After being cooled, the preform is inspected with a laser for any possible flaws. If perfect, the preform is reheated in a special furnace to 2,200° C. The preform melts and can be drawn into a gossamer-thin optical fiber. The fiber is immediately coated with plastic to protect it. A drawn optical fiber may be up to six miles long. The fiber is wound onto a spool and tested by quality control engineers before being stored.

Though an optical fiber looks fragile, it is stronger than steel and can withstand over 600,000 pounds of pulling force per square inch. Unlike ordinary glass, optical fibers are not brittle or easily broken.

An optical fiber is being drawn from a draw tower.

(Corning, Inc.)

An optical fiber is flexible enough to be tied into a loose knot and still transmit laser light flawlessly.

In the early 1970s solid state semiconductor diode lasers emerged. They are made from crystals of gallium arsenide. These crystals are smaller than the head of a pin, so small in fact that scientists joke about accidentally inhaling them. These tiny crystals have polished facets that take the place of the resonating mirrors of larger lasers. A semiconductor diode laser generates a continuous beam of laser light and can be joined with a hair-thin optical fiber. It is the laser used in most fiber optic communications systems today.

Sound and Data Transmission

How is your voice or information transmitted as pulses of light through optical fibers? The pattern of sound waves generated by your voice becomes a pattern of waves of electricity in the mouthpiece of a telephone. In an ordinary telephone, the waves of electricity then travel through copper wire to their destination. However, in a fiber optic system, a device known as an *encoder* measures the waves of electricity 8,000 times each second. The encoder then converts each measurement of the electrical waves into a series of eight ON-OFF pulses of infrared laser light. The optical signals are produced by a tiny semiconductor laser diode.

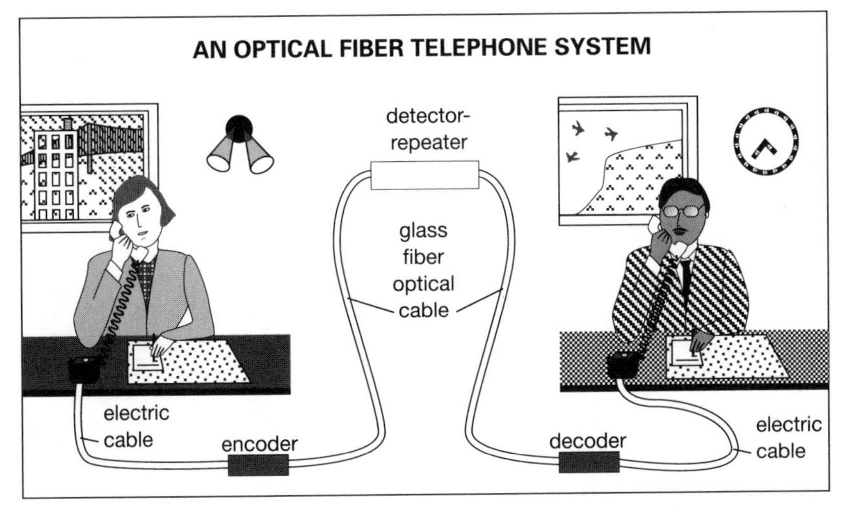

Figure 7

The laser pulses are *digitized,* or converted into a *binary code* that represents the sampled waves of electricity originally generated by your voice. A binary code uses only two signals or digits. Zero represents when the light pulse is OFF and one represents when the light pulse is ON.

The word *binary* means two and each zero or one is called a *bi*nary digi*t* or *bit.* A *byte* is eight bits grouped together. A digitized fiber optic telephone system can switch ON and OFF hundreds of millions of times each second. Information transmitted over such a system has a *bit rate* of hundreds of *megabits* (MBITs) per second.

At the receiving end of a fiber optic telephone line is a *decoder.* This device converts the pulses of laser light back into electrical waves. The electrical waves are then changed into the sound waves of your voice in the receiver of the telephone. Along the way, detector-repeater units amplify the laser beam before it passes through the next segment of optical fiber.

CHART OF TWO CODES THAT USE BINARY SYMBOLS

Pulses of ON/OFF laser light can represent familar characters such as the letters of the alphabet or the sounds of our voices and allow communications over fiber optic lines between computers and between people. Morse Code uses the dot and dash as binary symbols.

Character	Morse Code	ASCII-8
a	. -	11100001
b	- . . .	11100010
c	- . - .	11100011
d	- . .	11100100
e	.	11100101
f	. . - .	11100110
g	- - .	11100111
h	. . . .	11101000
i	. .	11101001
j	. - - -	11101010
k	- . -	11101011
l	. - . .	11101100
m	- -	11101101
n	- .	11101110
o	- - -	11101111
p	. - - .	11110000
q	- - . -	11110001
r	. - .	11110010
s	. . .	11110011
t	-	11110100
u	. . -	11110101
v	. . . -	11110110
w	. - -	11110111
x	- . . -	11111000
y	- . - -	11111001
z	- - . .	11111010

Coded pulses of ON-OFF light in a fiber optic system use the same binary language as computers. Most computers store or process information as a binary code of zeros and ones. For this reason, pulses of laser light teamed with optical fibers allow nearly instantaneous communication of vast quantities of information over telephone lines to, from, and between computers, as well as people. As an example, the contents of *Webster's Unabridged Dictionary* can be transmitted entirely between two computers in less than six seconds!

In 1977 in Chicago, the first attempt was made to use an optical fiber system to transmit voice, data, and pictures. Two Bell Telephone Company office buildings and a third customer facility were connected by 24 glass optical fibers. The light-carrying fibers were snaked through already existent telephone cables under the streets. The total length of the fibers used in this system was about one and one-half miles.

The Chicago system proved to be a model of efficiency. During the first 10 months of operation, it was only out of service for 20 seconds. Typical copper wire systems are out of operation for about two hours each year. In addition, the accuracy of transmission of information was over 99 percent.

The first commercial application of lasers and optical fibers to connect telephones in the United States was in 1978 at Disney World in Orlando, Florida. Vista-United Telecommunications linked telephones throughout the thousands of acres of the park using fiber optic trunk lines. In addition, alarm systems and lighting systems in the park use optical fibers.

Information booths in EPCOT (Experimental Prototype Community of Tomorrow) Center have television-like, two-way video screens and speakers. The system is activated by touching the screen. A visitor then can select from a menu of information that is shown on the screen, talk to an operator to ask directions, or make reservations at a restaurant in the park. An American Telephone and Telegraph (AT&T) trunk line over 780 miles long connects Boston; New York City; Washington, D.C.; and Richmond, Virginia. In this system, a fiber optic cable the thickness of an ordinary garden hose carries over 80,000 calls at one time.

In 1988, AT&T installed a fiber optic cable called TAT-8 under the ocean between North America and Europe. The name TAT-8 denotes that it is AT&T's eighth *t*rans*a*tlantic *t*elephone cable. A copper cable called TAT-1 was completed in 1956 and could carry 51 calls at one time. The last copper cable laid in 1983, TAT-7, transmits 8,000 calls at once. In comparison, TAT-8 carries 40,000 calls at one time.

Are Solitions a Solution?

Recently a physicist at Bell Laboratories has worked on some new ways to transmit laser pulses through long distances of optical fibers such as those needed for undersea cables. Dr. Linn F. Mollenauer has been studying light waves that do not alter their shape, even when traveling over long distances. These special kinds of waves are called *solitions.* In the early 1980s, he also invented a laser that emits light of strong enough intensity and in the correct frequency range to produce solition pulses.

At the same time, optical fibers were developed with a core small enough to carry the solitions over long distances. In February 1988, Mollenauer and his team of scientists transmitted light pulses through a coiled optical fiber 4,000 kilometers long without needing to regenerate the pulses. This is equivalent to the distance between New York and Los Angeles.

In 1989 there was a breaktrough. Scientists found that by coating optical fibers with the rare element erbium, the fibers would act as their own amplifiers when light was directed onto the fibers. In April 1991, with this improvement and using solition lasers and the erbium coated self-amplifying optical fibers, Mollenauer transmitted 2.5 gigabits of information over 7,500 kilometers. (A gigabit is 1 billion bits.) This is approximately the distance that pulses would need to travel in an undersea cable between North America and Europe. The improved technology could eliminate the need for expensive regeneration equipment.

HI-OVIS is the name of an optical fiber communications network near Tokyo, Japan. Its name stands for *H*ighly *I*nteractive *O*ptical *V*isual *I*nformation *S*ystem. This is a two-way system that allows people to participate in educational classes; get timely weather reports and news; and access airline, train, and concert schedules.

Advantages of Fiber Optic Communications

There are many advantages to an optical fiber communications system. The electrical signals carried in conventional copper wire telephone lines are sometimes bothered by interference from other electrical equipment, lightning storms, or power lines. This can cause static and other noise on a telephone line, the "poor connection" we have all experienced at one time or another. Light waves are unaffected by nearby electrical equipment, so sound is transmitted without interference.

The installation of fiber optic telephone lines is less costly than copper wire systems. The optical fibers only need repeaters to amplify

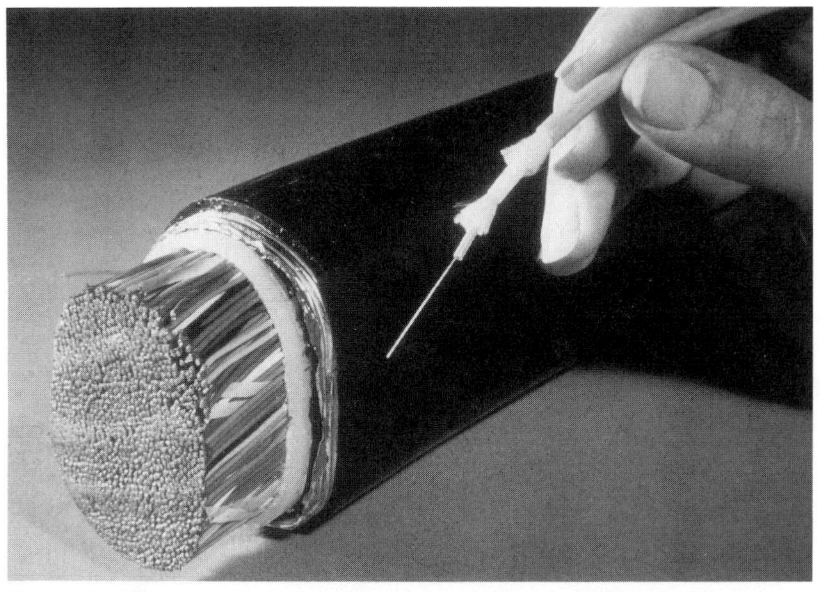

(Corning, Inc.)

One optical fiber can carry as much information as the 256 pairs of copper wires shown with it.

the signals every six miles or so. In a copper wire system, repeaters are needed every mile along the line to boost the signals. In addition, because as much information can be carried on a single pair of threadlike optical fibers as on a bundle of 256 pairs of copper wires, the optical fiber systems require less space. The optical fiber systems also are lighter and easier for workers to handle.

For the transmission of vital or secret information, optical fiber communications systems are superior to copper wire systems. For example, military information cannot be jammed or intercepted without being detected. And transmission lines that have been installed cannot be located by an enemy with metal detectors as can a copper wire system. The optical fiber systems can also be put in place near ammunition or fuel storage areas without fear of creating sparks, as could happen with electricity flowing through copper wires.

The communications facilities at the Kennedy Space Center in Florida use optical fibers. This includes the space shuttle control center and operations buildings for the launch complexes. The computers of the North American Air Defense Command located in Cheyenne Mountain in Colorado are linked by optical fibers and process radar information from around the world. In addition, the U.S. Army uses optical fibers in its field communications systems.

Many universities are installing fiber optic systems to interconnect campus computers. At the University of Pittsburgh, students can access information from other computers, classrooms, or the library through a fiber optic network that has been installed for that purpose.

Clearly, the combined technologies of lasers and optical fibers have vastly expanded our world of communications.

7 LASERS ARE REVOLUTIONIZING SURGERY

One of the most important uses of lasers today is for surgery. Lasers have truly revolutionized many traditional operations as well as making possible completely new surgical treatments. Several serious conditions of the human eye, including cataracts, glaucoma, and various kinds of retinal damage, can cause blindness. Many of these conditions can now be corrected with laser surgery. Lasers also are enabling surgeons to perform many kinds of operations on almost any part of the human anatomy with far less trauma and discomfort to the patient.

Laser Eye Surgery: Restoring the Gift of Sight

Lasers are precise instruments that can be used to reach tissues deep inside the eye without cutting or disturbing other parts of the eye. The smallest ordinary scalpel makes cuts that are as wide as the tip of a pin and that crush adjacent tissues. A laser beam can slice as thinly as the width of one cell. And because the instrument does not actually touch the delicate surgical site, it does not damage neighboring tissues. The laser pulses are so rapid—perhaps as many as one thousand in a second—that the patient does not have time to blink or feel pain.

Ophthalmologists who perform eye surgery view the pupil of the eye as a natural window through which a laser beam can enter. Because the eye itself does not need to be cut open, the risks of infection and pain are lessened. Usually laser surgery on the eye can be done right in the doctor's office or at the outpatient department of a hospital. Most patients can go back to normal activities the same day.

A serious eye disease called *cataracts* is a clouding of the normally clear or transparent lens of the eye. One patient described the symptoms as, "like looking through a window with soap on it."

Traditional cataract surgery replaces the natural lens of the eye with an artificial one. A microscopic semicircular cut is made at the edge of the lens capsule. The lens is gently replaced and the opening closed with tiny sutures.

In some cataract patients the back portion of the membrane that encloses the replacement lens may become cloudy several months after the original surgery. In the procedure known as a *posterior capsulotomy,* a dozen or so one-billionth-of-a-second blasts of intense infrared light from the neodymium:yttrium aluminum garnet (Nd:YAG) laser create an opening in the clouded membrane that restores clear eyesight.

In this follow-up form of cataract surgery, only the precisely focused tip of the infrared laser beam has enough energy to vaporize the cloudy cells while the other tissues of the eye remain unharmed. There are no nerve endings in the membrane behind the lens of the eye, so the procedure is painless for the patient.

Glaucoma is a disease that affects two out of every 100 Americans over the age of 35, according to the American Academy of Ophthalmology. It is a leading cause of blindness in the United States. The disease is characterized by a build-up of excessive fluid pressure in the eye. Normally the clear fluid of the inner eye flows continuously through open canals. In a glaucoma patient, these canals become blocked and fluids accumulate. Untreated, the excessive fluid pressure causes damage to the *optic nerve,* the nerve pathway that conducts the images of what we see to the brain for interpretation.

An ophthalmologist can use the beam from a Nd:YAG laser to make an opening that allows fluids in the inner eye to drain. Relieving excessive pressure on the optic nerve prevents the damage that causes blindness from glaucoma.

Macular degeneration is a disease that is the most common cause of blindness in people over 65 years of age. It already affects several million Americans and as the average age of the population of the United States gets older, it is becoming more prevalent.

The back inside wall of the human eye is lined with a delicate, light-sensitive tissue called the *retina.* The images we see are formed on the retina and nerves that can sense the image send the information through the optic nerve to the brain.

The most sensitive portion of the retina is the *macula.* It is 100 times more sensitive to visual detail than other portions of the retina. And though it is less than one-tenth of an inch in diameter, the macula is

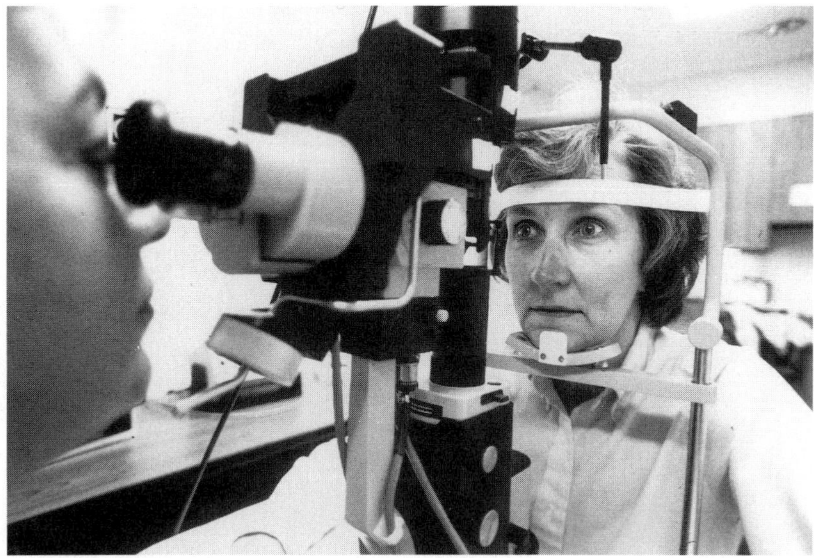
(U.S. Food and Drug Administration)

A patient is prepared for laser surgery on her eye.

vital to the straight-ahead vision needed to see properly when doing fine work such as reading small print or sewing, driving a car, or even recognizing a person's face.

Macular degeneration destroys central vision. People with this disease suffer a gradual loss of sharp, focused, central vision while their peripheral or side vision remains intact. The result is that straight lines appear crooked or distorted and a blurry, darkened area appears in the center of the patient's vision.

There are two forms of macular degeneration. One is called the *dry form* and no treatment currently is available. However, about 10 percent of the patients with macular degeneration have a *wet form* of the disease. For reasons unknown, in this form of the disease, new blood vessels grow underneath the retina. The new blood vessels sometimes leak, causing damage and scarring the macula.

With early detection, cases of wet form macular degeneration often can be helped with argon laser surgery. The green argon laser beam is absorbed especially well by red objects, including red blood cells. The beam heats tissue, rather than vaporizing it. Thus the laser beam *photocoagulates*, or seals, the abnormal blood vessels to stop the leakage that would lead to irreversible damage to the macula.

In patients who do not have many abnormal blood vessels scattered behind the macula, the narrowness of the argon laser beam allows the

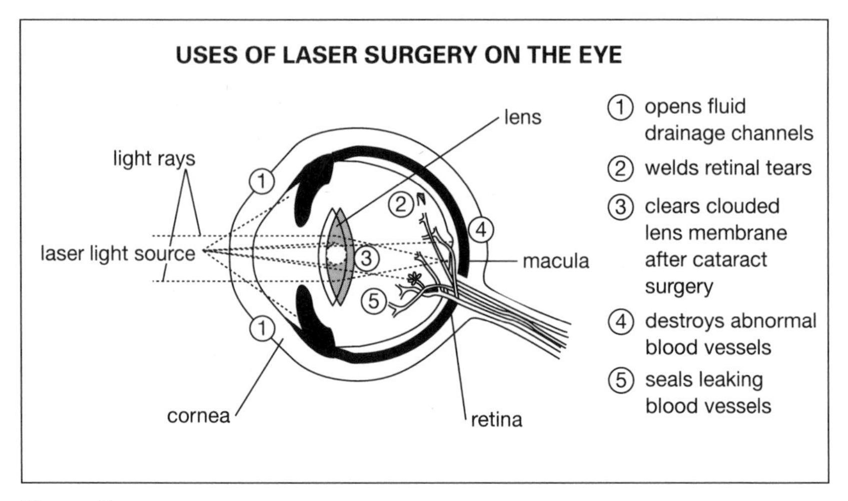

Figure 8

surgeon to treat only the abnormal blood vessels without disturbing most of the retina or other parts of the eye. The surgery only takes a few minutes and may require only a local anesthetic.

In about three out of four wet form macula degeneration patients, however, the proliferation of abnormal blood vessels behind the macula is so scattered that the ophthalmologist is uncertain about where to aim the laser beam. Each time the laser beam strikes the retina, it destroys a tiny bit of the membrane. When the abnormal blood vessels are too scattered, argon laser treatment may cause too much damage to the patient's vision to make it advisable.

Two researchers at Johns Hopkins University School of Medicine have been tackling this difficult problem. Neil M. Bressler and Susan B. Bressler have tried using krypton and tunable dye lasers to apply experimental treatments in a gridlike pattern on the retina. The laser beam hits the retina in microscopically small pinpoints that are only 150 microns apart. The pegboardlike pattern of treatment zaps a significant number of the abnormal blood vessels while leaving most of the retina unharmed.

The Bresslers are encouraged by the results of trials of this treatment on their patients. In some of their patients, leakage from abnormal blood vessels was completely stopped. Nevertheless, many more patients must receive this experimental treatment before its usefulness can be proven.

In addition to age-related macular degeneration, a disease called *ocular histoplasmosis* also can cause abnormal growth of blood vessels behind the retina that can damage the macula. The disease occurs in the southeastern and midwestern parts of the United States where a fungus that causes it is present. If detection and laser treatment are done early, serious loss of vision can be prevented. Estimates are that about 2,000 cases could be treated successfully by argon laser each year if the disease is detected before great damage has occurred to the macula.

Another leading cause of blindness is *diabetic retinopathy.* According to the National Eye Institute, almost half of all people with diabetes suffer at least mild diabetic retinopathy. As the disease advances, people with diabetes may develop faulty blood vessels on or within the retina. When these bleed, the patient may suffer severe deterioration and scarring of the retina. Again, prompt treatment with an argon laser can halt the bleeding and stop the patient's vision loss.

Argon lasers are also useful to repair *retinal detachments* and *tears.* Retinal detachments occur when a portion of the retina pulls away from the supporting membrane at the back of the eye. Retinal tears are horseshoe-shaped holes in the retina. Either may be caused by an accident or a blow to the head. The detachments or tears disrupt normal vision and may bleed into the fluid-filled central portion of the eye. Both argon and krypton lasers are heat producing and can be used to spot-weld the retina back into place and to stop the bleeding.

The transparent front covering of the eye is called the *cornea.* Light entering the normal eye is bent by the cornea and the lens of the eye so that the image it forms is in clear focus when it strikes the retina at the back of the eye. However, many individuals are nearsighted, farsighted, or have astigmatism. For these reasons, they need to wear glasses or contact lenses to correct their vision.

Nearsighted people have trouble seeing distant objects. Light rays entering their eyes come to focus in front of their retina instead of directly on its light-sensitive surface. This condition results because the curvature of the lens or the cornea of their eye is too steep or because their eyeball is too long. Farsightedness is just the opposite. People who are farsighted have trouble clearly seeing objects that are close to them. In this case, the curvature of the cornea or lens is not steep enough or the eyeball is too short. Light entering the eye is focused behind the retina instead of directly on its surface.

In a procedure called *radial keratotomy,* a traditional scalpel is used to make several small incisions in the cornea. The tiny slits allow the curvature of the cornea to slightly flatten. The hoped-for effect is to correct the patient's nearsightedness. However, a study published in the February 22, 1990, issue of the *Journal of the American Medical*

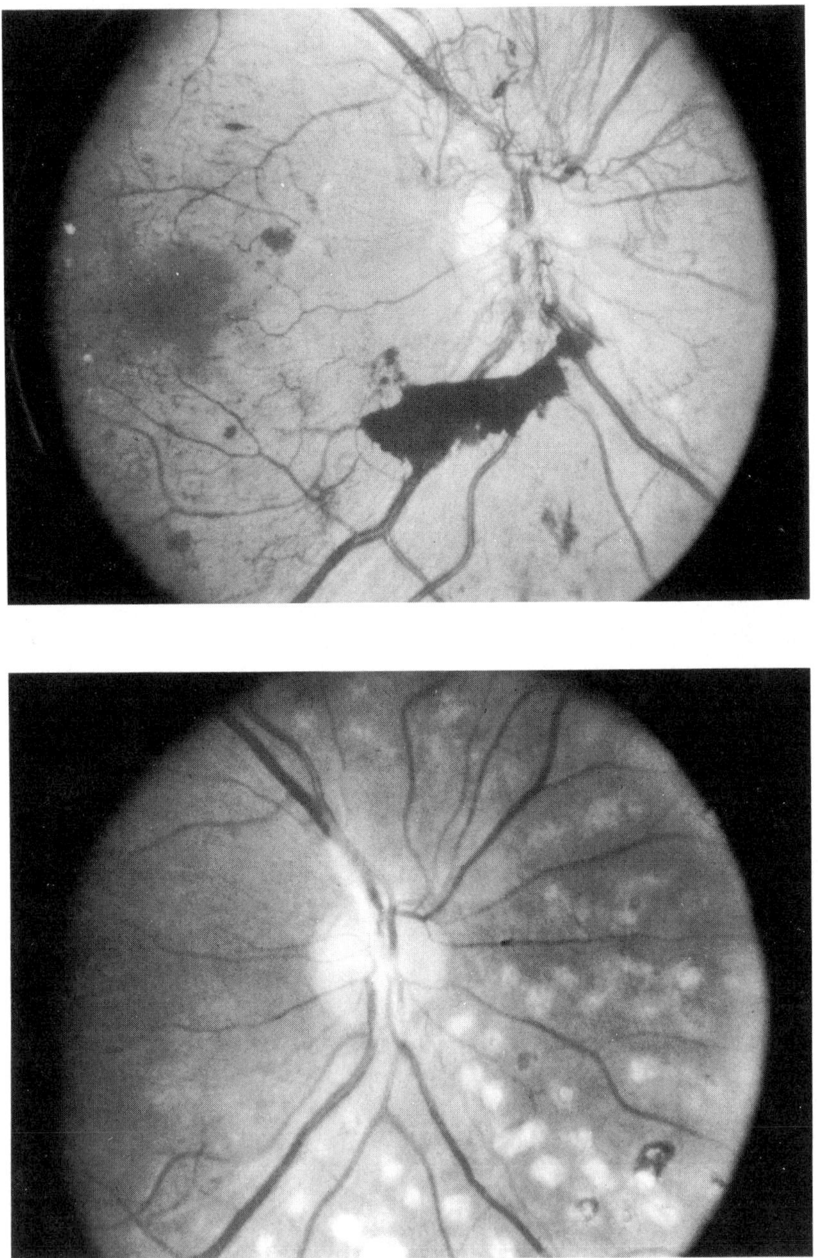

(Marjorie Mosier, M.D., Beckman Laser Institute & Medical Clinic)

Diabetic retinopathy can now be treated with lasers. The photo on the top shows the eye before laser treatment; the photo on the bottom shows it afterward.

Association, states that in almost half of all cases, the treated eyes are either undercorrected or overcorrected.

The problems encountered with radial keratotomy seem to happen because the hand-held scalpel cannot make cuts of adequately consistent size and shape. In addition, scar tissue that forms during healing may alter the intended final shape of the cornea.

Although still considered experimental, cool ultraviolet excimer lasers have been used to reshape the surface of the cornea of one eye in nearsighted people. The procedure is called *photo-refractive keratectomy* (PRK). (Doing the other eye awaits approval of the procedure by the Food and Drug Administration [FDA]). Cuts made with this high energy kind of laser beam can remove cell-sized bits of tissue without producing heat. The resultant slits in the cornea are precisely placed and exactly uniform. And because the excimer laser does far less damage to surrounding tissue, the formation of scar tissue during healing is minimized.

The actual surgical reshaping of the cornea with an excimer laser takes less than one minute and is painless. At Louisiana State University Eye Center in New Orleans, the preparation time is about 15 minutes. After the patient is lightly sedated, a computer linked to the laser is programmed with the shape of the individual's cornea.

The physician uses the excimer laser to make the required number of perfectly placed slits in the cornea to complete the operation. The

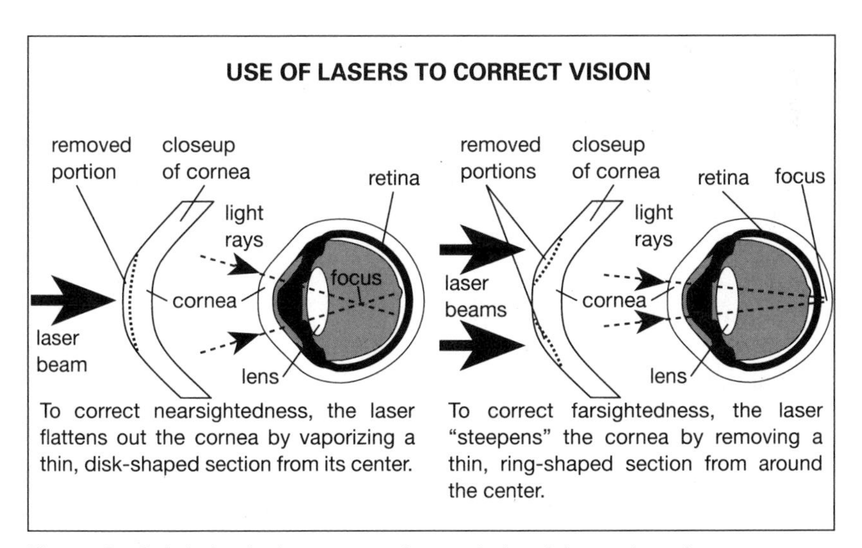

Figure 9: *Ophthalmologists are testing cool ultraviolet excimer lasers to correct nearsightedness. A modification of the technique also can be used to treat farsightedness.*

cornea may ache for a day after the procedure and an eye patch is needed for 24 to 48 hours after the surgery.

Researchers at Johns Hopkins University in Baltimore as well as at Louisiana State University (LSU) Eye Center have treated nearsighted patients with excimer laser sculpting. Though experimental results seem encouraging, more studies must be completed to confirm the effectiveness and safety of the procedure. Dr. Walter J. Stark at the Johns Hopkins University School of Medicine says the widespread use of lasers to correct nearsightedness and farsightedness is still futuristic because early studies indicate that the sculpted corneas tend to revert back to their old shape.

Dr. Stark reports that several people have been treated successfully with an excimer laser for corneal scars. In some patients, the only alternative would be a corneal transplant, an expensive operation that lacks adequate donors of healthy corneas.

Further in the future, Marguerite McDonald at the LSU Eye Center says that it may be possible to sculpt corneas so that they can focus on far away objects at the top and close up objects on the bottom—creating a kind of bifocal eyeball.

Astigmatism is caused by tiny pits and bumps on the surface of the cornea. Vision is blurred because the irregularities on the corneal surface bend light rays entering the eye and prevent them from forming a sharply focused image on the retina.

Scientists in the United States and in Berlin, Germany, are trying excimer laser surgery on patients to smooth out the bumps and pits on their corneas that cause their astigmatism. A series of T-shaped incisions made with the laser may prove to be effective in smoothing the corneal irregularities. Not all results are yet reported and further clinical trials are needed before this procedure can become standard practice.

Other Kinds of Surgery

One of the most common lasers used in surgery is the carbon dioxide gas laser. It produces an infrared laser beam with a wavelength that is completely absorbed by water. Living tissue consists mostly of water, so it absorbs the beam readily even at low powers. The heat produced vaporizes or burns away the tissue in the path of the laser beam.

The carbon dioxide gas laser beam can be controlled precisely to remove only a few surface cells or to cut deeper into the tissue. Its beam can be focused to cut a line as fine as one cell in width. Because little damage is done to surrounding tissues, healing is often faster than with conventional surgery.

In addition, the searing heat produced by the absorption of the carbon dioxide laser beam seals off blood vessels as the cutting proceeds, so very little bleeding occurs. In many operations this may mean that blood transfusions that would have been necessary with ordinary surgery are not needed.

Another great advantage to the infrared carbon dioxide laser beam is that it is invisible. The surgeon has an unobstructed view of the incision as it is being made. An ordinary scalpel and other similar surgical tools block at least some portion of the surgeon's view.

In practice, the operating physician is provided with a microscope that greatly magnifies the view of the area undergoing surgery. A visible light beam also can be used as a guide to indicate the location where the incision is to be made by the infrared laser beam. Mirrors can reflect and direct the laser beam through the rigid, articulated arms of the carbon dioxide laser to the surgical site.

The carbon dioxide gas laser is used by dermatologists (specialists in diseases of the skin) to remove warts, various kinds of lesions, birthmarks such as port wine stains, and tattoos. More of the laser beam is absorbed by the pigmented areas of the skin while little change occurs in the normal skin. The depth of the carbon dioxide laser beam can be precisely controlled to preserve underlying tissue.

Physicians specializing in diseases of the ear, nose, mouth, and throat (otolaryngology) also utilize the carbon dioxide laser for surgery. One application is in treating abnormal wartlike growths called papillomas on the larynx or voice box. With the laser, the surgery can be accomplished with great precision and because underlying tissue is not damaged, often can restore the patient's normal voice.

Small cancerous tumors on the vocal cords can be treated with radiation therapy. However, if they recur radiation treatment cannot be repeated. Recurrence may now mean removal of half or more of the voice box. The laser often can cure these small tumors and if they do recur, treatment can safely be repeated. The patient's larynx and voice may be saved.

Surgeons also use the carbon dioxide gas laser to remove lesions in the bronchus or windpipe and some of its main branches to the lungs, as well as in the esophagus, the tube leading from the mouth to the stomach.

Tonsils are sometimes removed using a laser. Small growths that may form on tonsils also can be treated with the laser. Patients with chronic infection of the tonsils also can be treated with the laser, sometimes preventing the need to remove them.

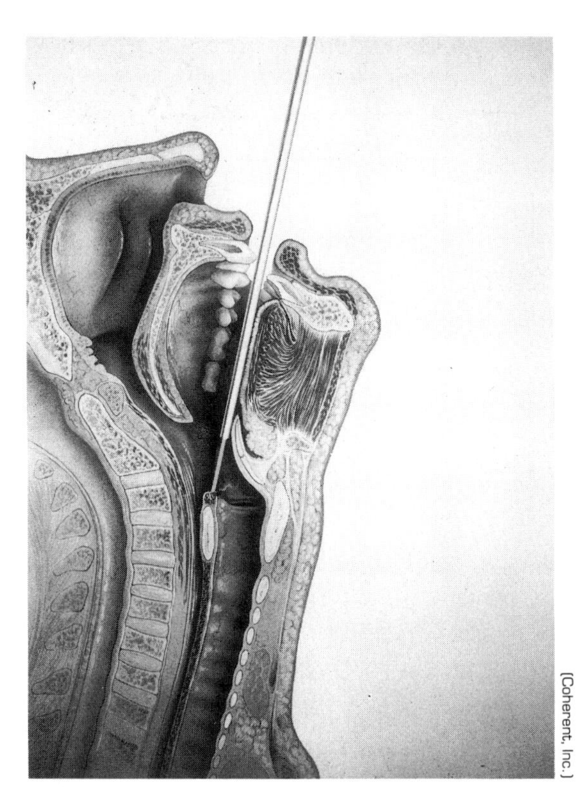

(Coherent, Inc.)

Lasers can be used to perform throat surgery.

Neurosurgeons have found that using a combination of traditional surgical instruments and the carbon dioxide gas laser to remove noncancerous tumors occurring near the base of the brain poses less risk to the patient. Conventional instruments are used to gain access to the surgical site. Then the carbon dioxide gas laser is used to remove the tumor itself. The precision of the laser causes less disruption of neighboring areas of the brain, thus lessening possible side effects such as blindness, paralysis, or loss of coordination. Combinations of traditional and laser surgery also are being used to treat cancerous and noncancerous tumors of the spinal cord.

The carbon dioxide gas laser is used by gynecologists to treat conditons that affect a woman's reproductive system. Whereas with conventional surgery some conditions used to require removal of an organ, with laser surgery, lesions often can be treated without removal. An example is the treatment of precancerous or cancerous lesions that may occur on the cervix, the narrow lower portion of the uterus or womb.

Another condition that affects many women is *endometriosis.* Tissue similar to that which normally lines the uterus grows on the

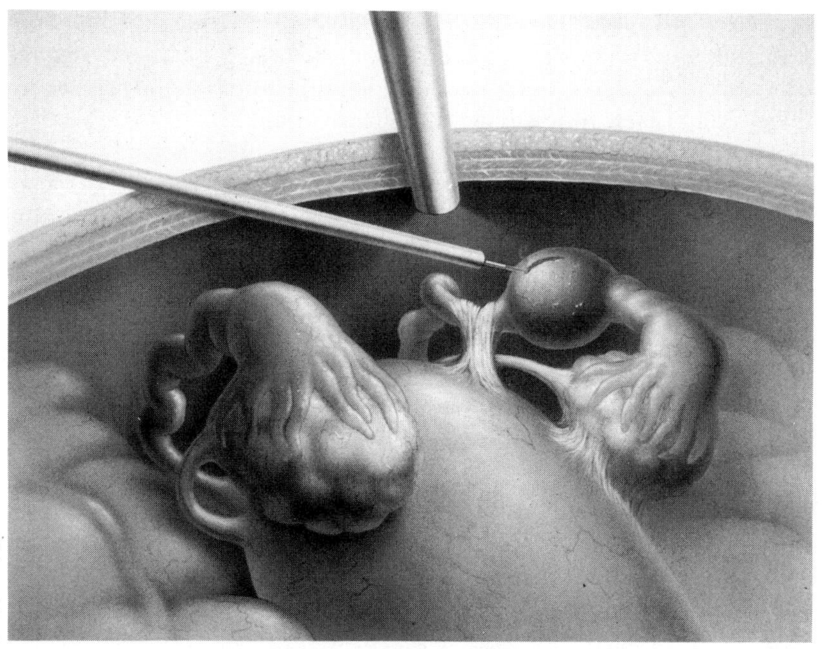

(Coherent, Inc.)

Surgery to treat endometriosis can now be done with a laser rather than a scalpel.

surfaces of the ligaments, ovaries, or the intestines in the abdominal cavity. Lasers have been successfully used to treat this often painful disease.

Orthopedic surgeons have not used lasers extensively because the carbon dioxide and Nd:YAG lasers are not capable of effectively cutting bone. However, when combined with an arthroscope (a small endoscope designed for use on the knee and other joints), a laser can be used to remove damaged or diseased cartilage (uncalcified bone).

Podiatrists, or foot doctors, use the carbon dioxide gas laser to correct conditions such as ingrown toenails, plantar warts on the bottom of the foot, and other growths. It is also used to release blood that has accumulated under nails after an injury.

In general, the carbon dioxide gas laser is a surgical tool that is used for tissue removal and for controlled cutting as a "bloodless" scalpel.

The Nd:YAG laser is being used increasingly to remove cancerous tumors that block the airways to the lungs. In addition, some attempts have been made to combine radiation therapy with the Nd:YAG laser treatment. Nd:YAG lasers are being utilized to remove one form of tumor that occurs in the urinary bladder. *Transition-cell carcinoma,* as it is called, does not spread very much, but it does have a high rate of recurrence. The conventional treatment for this form of bladder cancer is done with electrosurgical instruments. Surgeons who have tried using Nd:YAG laser treatment for this cancer have reported a lower rate of recurrence than with electrosurgery.

With large bladder tumors, a combination of electrosurgery and laser treatment is sometimes used. The electrosurgery removes most of the tumor, and then the laser is used to try to destroy any remaining cancer cells on the inside of the bladder wall.

Gastroenterologists are physicians who specilize in the treatment of diseases of the digestive tract. A flexible fiber optic endoscope can be used like a spyglass, capable of reaching most segments of the digestive tract without the need for conventional surgery. With an endoscopically equipped Nd:YAG laser, the physician can gain access to all of the digestive tract except for some portions of the small intestine.

A variety of benign, or noncancerous, growths, such as certain polyps that may develop into tumors if not treated, can be removed with the Nd:YAG laser outfitted with an endoscope. Large tumors that can completely block the esophagus or large intestine can be removed as well. This is especially important in advanced cancer cases, mainly to open the passageway rather than to cure the patient.

Sometimes an accumulation of blood vessels similar to a port-wine stain occurs in the digestive tract. If this abnormality bleeds, it can be treated with the laser. Swollen veins that may occur in the esophagus usually are treated with medications. But some patients cannot use the medications and in these cases laser treatment is used instead.

Patients with bleeding ulcers often have lost so much blood that they cannot risk conventional surgery. However, an Nd:YAG laser outfitted with an endoscope can probe to the site of the ulcer. The laser's beam stops the bleeding by coagulating the blood vessels surrounding the ulcer. In half the cases, this is sufficient to cure the patient. If not, with the bleeding stopped, the blood supply can be replenished with transfusions, giving the patient a better chance to survive traditional surgery.

New laser tip designs offer additional ways to treat some patients. One laser tip consists of a bundle of optical fibers. It is not as highly focused as a conventional laser tip but is easier to control. Other laser tips convert the energy of the laser beam into heat. These are being explored to open up clogged arteries with the hope that they eventually can be used to clear the coronary arteries that are critical to supply blood to the heart itself.

Sapphire contact tips have been designed to make incisions for treatment of tumors in organs such as the liver. Surgery on the liver is very difficult because of the risk of bleeding or unintended injury to its soft tissue, which has many blood vessels.

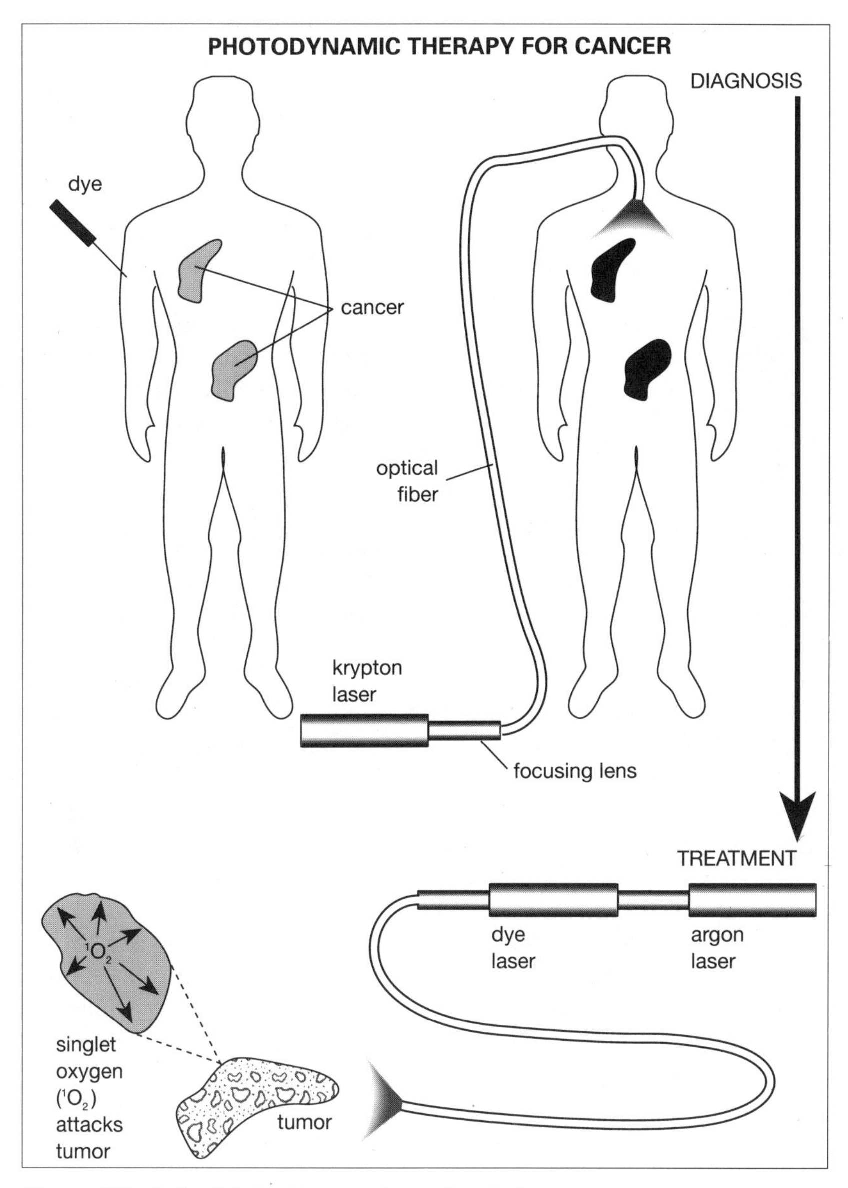

Figure 10: *A dye injected two or three days before treatment concentrates in cancerous tissue. Blue-violet light from a krypton laser travels through an optical fiber to the site of the malignant growth. The laser light makes the tumor fluoresce so the physician can easily see it and make a diagnosis. Then another wavelength of laser light is used to excite the dye molecules in the tumor, which pass their energy to oxygen molecules. The excited oxygen, called singlet oxygen, destroys the cancer.*

Another laser technique for treatment of various cancers is called *photodynamic therapy,* or PDT. This treatment uses a dye laser in combination with a light-absorbing drug such as *hematoporphyrin deritive,* or HpD. HpD is a product of hemoglobin, the protein that gives blood its red color. It strongly absorbs red light, which can be emitted by a dye laser.

The patient is injected with HpD two or three days before laser therapy. The HpD concentrates in the cancerous cells. Later when laser light is directed at the cancerous cells, they are destroyed, leaving neighboring normal cells intact. This technique is being tried by investigators on cancerous tumors of the bladder, uterus, pharynx (connects the mouth to the esophagus), and bronchial tubes.

The combination of HpD and laser light also is being tested as a diagnostic tool. HpD fluoresces when certain wavelengths of light strike it. For example, a researcher may try to learn if a suspected bronchial tube tumor is present. If the patient is injected with HpD and then exposed to red laser light, the tumor may fluoresce and reveal itself at an early, otherwise undetectable stage of growth. Early detection increases the chance of successful removal and return to good health.

Various lasers and techniques are now being tried to treat *atherosclerosis,* or arteries clogged with cholesterol deposits that have hardened into patches of plaque. The excimer laser produces a high-energy, short-duration pulse of ultraviolet light with a shorter wavelength than an argon laser. Some researchers have reported that it seems safe to reopen blocked arteries. And it is especially good at removing hardened plaque from inside walls of arteries.

Sometimes the removal of plaque in an artery with a laser is assisted by a procedure called *balloon angioplasty.* A slim hollow tube known as a *catheter* and containing a deflated balloon at its tip is inserted into the artery. When the tip of the tube reaches the site where the plaque was removed, the balloon is inflated to open the artery further. Then the balloon is deflated and the catheter removed.

In addition to other attempts to use lasers to reopen clogged arteries, a "smart" laser has been developed. This laser uses a computer to help identify different kinds of tissue based upon its fluorescence. The "smart" laser consists of a computer, a low-power diagnostic laser, a high-power treatment laser, and an optical fiber to deliver the laser energy.

The optical fiber is threaded into the clogged artery to the site of the blockage. The low-power diagnostic laser is fired and the computer analyzes and identifies the tissue as plaque, a blood clot, or part of the artery wall. If it is plaque or a clot, the treatment laser is used to vaporize the tissue. The advantage of the "smart" laser is that it avoids damaging healthy tissue that underlies the plaque or clot. The U.S. Food and Drug Adminstration (FDA) approved the "smart" laser for clinical trials in 1988. It has shown an excellent success rate in preliminary patients.

A technique called *direct laser revascularization* is being tried. In some patients who undergo a coronary bypass, portions of their heart muscle will not benefit from the surgery. On a trial basis, in a few of these cases, tiny channels are being created with the laser that allow the heart muscle to get blood directly from the ventricle, or pumping chamber, of the heart. The experimental results have been encouraging.

Whether restoring eyesight, curing a cancerous tumor, unclogging an artery, treating endometriosis, removing a diseased gallbladder, or erasing a birthmark, lasers have made possible more precise, improved techniques of surgery. Because damage to surrounding tissue is minimized with laser surgery, patients lose less blood, experience less discomfort, and recover more quickly than from traditional surgical techniques. Surgical lasers produce beams that heal.

8 DENTISTS LIGHTEN UP

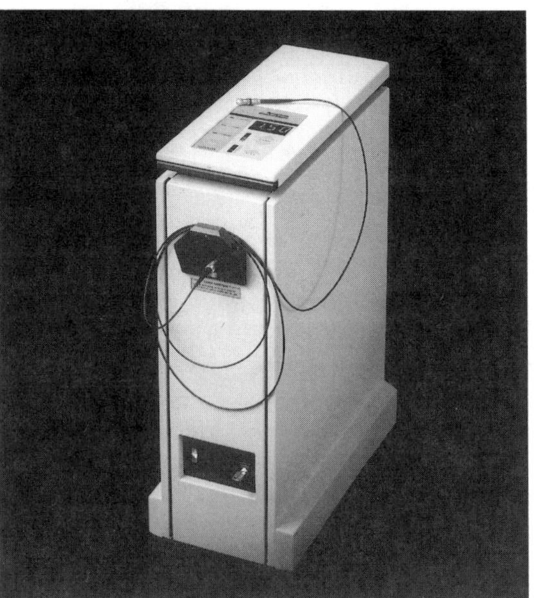
(American Dental Laser)

Dentistry is one of many fields to take up the use of lasers.

Another area of medicine in which lasers are being used is dentistry. Dr. Terry Myers of Birmingham, Michigan, has designed a three watt, pulsed, Nd:YAG laser with a hand-held fiber optic tip for use in dentistry. The dental laser uses visible light as a guiding beam while an invisible laser beam does the work. Dr. Myers's Nd:YAG laser has also been used in Canada, England, Japan, Mexico, Belgium, Guatemala, Italy, Turkey, Singapore, Switzerland, and Australia. Hundreds of dentists in the United States are using it. Its 1.064 micron laser beam is capable of destroying the retina of the eyes, so both the patient and the dentist must wear special protective goggles that filter out the Nd:YAG beam while the laser is in use.

Painless Dentistry

As an example, a procedure known as *laser subgingival curettage* removes diseased gum tissue. The dentist presses a foot control to activate the laser, which pulses 10 to 30 times each second. Each pulse lasts only millionths of a second, vaporizing the diseased gum tissue without harming the healthy tissue underneath.

The patient hears what sounds like tiny firecrackers popping but feels no pain because the laser pulses are too short to trigger a neural response. The laser pulses not only vaporize diseased tissue, they destroy any disease-causing bacteria that are present.

If the equivalent surgery were done by the conventional means of scraping the gum with a surgical blade, the patient would need to have an anesthetic during the procedure and might have difficulty eating for weeks afterward. The pain after a gum operation and the time needed to heal are significantly reduced by using laser surgery.

Dr. Delwin McCarthy was one of the first dentists in the United States to use the laser experimentally. He says,

> *With the laser we can clean out diseased pockets of gum tissue to the point where the body can heal itself. We can also make the teeth more resistant to future decay by sterilizing the deep crevices toothbrushes can't reach.*

Another use for the dental laser is in the treatment of sores in the mouth. Many patients have almost instantaneous relief from the pain of abcesses, canker sores, viral lesions, denture sores, and small noncancerous tumors after laser treatment.

In another application, the dental laser is used to desensitize exposed tooth dentin. Patients may suffer from dentin hypersensitivity in areas where the enamel of their teeth no longer protects the dentin underneath, such as along receding gum lines. The laser treatment closes microscopic, tiny tubes in the dentin that lead to a network of nerves within the tooth.

The dental laser also is used to perform root canals. Dr. Robert M. Pick, a professor of periodontics at Northwestern University's dental school, says,

> *In root canal therapy, we can insert the laser fiber into the root canals, remove the infected tissue by vaporizing it, and destroy the bacteria causing the infection. I think this is going to be a great improvement over present techniques which are not totally effective in removing all the bacteria.*

Even when conventional dental surgery with a scalpel is necessary, the surfaces of cut tissue can be treated with a laser to reduce pain and often to eliminate the need to prescribe painkillers after surgery.

The *frenum* is a small bit of membrane that attaches the upper lip to the gum within the mouth. Sometimes the frenum can push teeth out of alignment. The laser can vaporize the frenum painlessly and without bleeding.

New Teeth from Old

Lasers are transforming the way dental crowns and bridges are made. The FDA has approved a computer-guided laser system for this purpose. The laser beam is guided around the tooth and the data it collects is fed into a computer. The computer then designs and controls the manufacturing of the crown.

9 LASER RECORDING

Compact disks (CDs) and *compact video disks* (CDVs) are revolutionary new ways of storing and transmitting sound, pictures, and information. The technology uses laser beams both to record or encode information onto compact disks and to "read" or play back the stored information.

CDs and CDVs

A compact disk resembles a phonograph record in some ways but is very different in others. For example, the groove on a phonograph record is a continuous spiral that is followed by the phonograph needle as the record plays from beginning to end. A compact disk encodes information or music in concentric circles with billions of bumps known as *pits.* The pits are etched onto the disk by a laser and later, when the disk is played, they interrupt a slim laser beam that shines on the disk as it plays.

The pits on a CD are only 0.00002 inch in width and 0.000004331 inch deep. The tiny pits are "read" by a very precise, narrow laser beam. Because the pits are so infinitesimally small, they can contain much more information in a smaller space. Within 33 millimeters of its radius, a five-and-one-quarter-inch CD contains over 20,000 tracks of pits. For this reason, CDs live up to their "compact" name and are only about one-sixth the size of a long-playing phonograph record. Up to 74 minutes of music or information can be recorded on one side of a CD.

As in fiber optic communication, the pits on a CD stand for information in the form of a binary code. The information, music, or video picture to be recorded onto the disk is digitized. In the case of music,

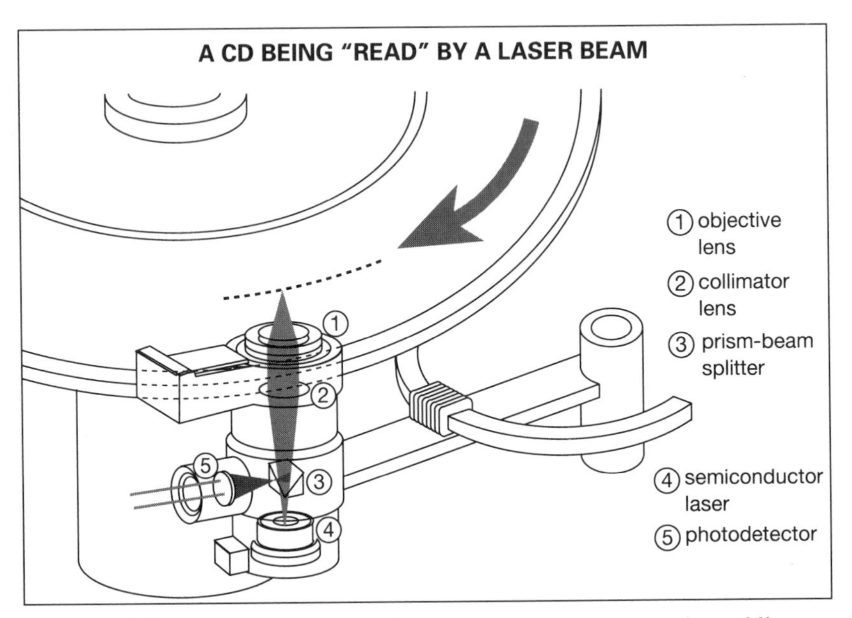

Figure 11: The output from a continuous wave semiconductor laser (4) passes through a prism-beam splitter (3) arrangement and is focused using the lens assembly (1) on to the surface of the moving disk. The light reflected from the etched surface, which contains the digital information, is collected by the lens system (2) and reflected off the beam splitter onto a photodetector (5).

the sound is sampled at the rate of 44,100 times each second (more than twice the highest audible frequency humans can hear—20,000 times per second) and each sample becomes 16 binary digits, or bits. If music is being recorded for two stereo channels, each second of sound represents 1.4 million bits of data on the CD. The awesome accuracy of recording sound on a CD is possible because of the billions of bits of information that it can hold.

When a CD is played, the laser beam shines on the disk from below and passes through a protective thin transparent layer on the disk to focus on an aluminum reflecting film or signal surface. At the surface where the pits are recorded, the diameter of the laser beam is a mere 1.7 micrometers. Even if the protective transparent layer on the CD becomes dusty or scratched, the laser beam is so finely focused that most of these do not affect playing quality because they are out of focus.

Compact disks are manufactured with a built-in error correction code. Errors may be random, such as those that occur during disk

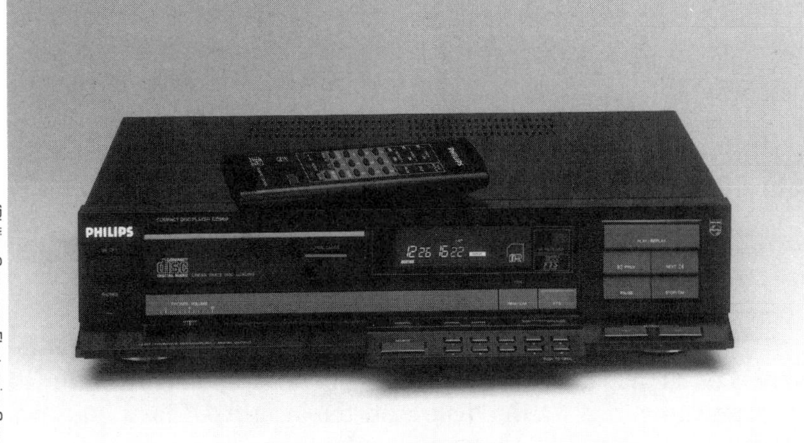

(Philips Consumer Electronics Company)

Philips CD player

production when the cutting of the disk or application of coating to a disk are inaccurate. Or errors can result from severe scratches or heavy dirt on the disk. Using a process called *interpolation,* incorrect bits of information are estimated from the preceding and succeeding blocks of bits of data.

The surface of a compact disk must be squarely perpendicular (at a 90° angle) to the laser beam that is reading it. Otherwise the sound will be distorted because the laser light will be skewed. Skew usually is due to a disk becoming warped by the absorption of moisture. For

(Philips Consumer Electronics Company)

Magnavox portable CD player

this reason, compact disks are injection-molded with a substance that makes them less susceptible to moisture damage.

Compact disk players play back the sound on a CD at a speed of 1.2 meters per second. To keep this speed constant, the turntable of the CD player rotates 458 revolutions per minute when the laser is "reading" near the center of the disk. As the laser beam moves outward, the turntable speed gradually slows to 197 revolutions per minute.

There are many advantages to CDs besides the clarity of sound. Because the laser "reads" the CD through the clear coating without coming into contact with the disk, CDs do not wear out as do conventional phonograph records played with a needle. In addition, there is no surface noise, no hiss, pops, or clicks, and no distortion of the sound from dirt on the disk. And the laser itself lasts 10 times longer than a diamond phonograph stylus.

CDVs are compact disks that record both sound and video. The 12-inch CDV also looks similar to a phonograph record but actually is very different. The information to be recorded is coded into microscopically small pits in concentric grooves on the CDV with a beam from an argon laser. In this case, the data must be recorded as three separate bands; two are needed for stereophonic sound and one is for the color video picture. As the CDV rotates at 1,800 revolutions per minute, a laser beam "reads" the pits on the disk and the encoded information is converted into electrical signals to reproduce the sound and color pictures recorded on the disk. The CDV is double bonded

A Pioneer CD LaserDisc player designed to play up to five CDs or a 12-inch LaserDisc for continuous audio and video playback

(Photograph reprinted with the permission of Pioneer Electronics [USA] Inc.)

(Videodiscovery, Inc.)

A student uses a video disk system to study biology.

to keep out damaging moisture. It has the same advantages of accuracy and long life as a CD.

Additional advantages of both CDs and CDVs are that the listener can jump from one song on a CD to another with great precision. In the case of CDVs the operator can return to the exact video frame and sound where he or she left off. Video disks contain features such as a table of contents with a listing of chapters so that the operator can find the exact desired location on the disk.

Laser Libraries and an Information-Rich Society

The number of products available for use based on compact disk storage is burgeoning. This new way of recording sound and video is used for entertainment. However, CDs also are a new way to store vast quantities of information in a read only memory (ROM).

Many libraries now offer computerized resources for students to do research. CDROM disks accompany a computer set up for this purpose in the library. For example, citations of articles that have appeared in recent magazines and journals are listed by subject area from a computerized data base that the student can call up from a menu on the computer screen.

Articles that contain information of interest to the student can be previewed on the computer screen. If the person then wants a copy of the article, it can be printed out directly from an available CDROM disk.

The computerized procedure saves many hours of time compared to manually looking up articles listed in resources such as *Readers' Guide to Periodical Literature* and then physically going to libraries to locate the article and copy the information needed. Computerized data bases also have an advantage of being periodically updated so that very recently published articles are available readily.

Many companies now offer long lists of specialized data bases. These laser libraries may include subject areas such as science and technology, biography, art, business periodicals, humanities, *Readers' Guide to Periodical Literature,* library literature, education, and social sciences to name a few. In addition, services are offered for computerized online access to the most current information and data.

Electronic Trend Publications of Saratoga, California, has analyzed the information storage market in a report titled *The Impact of Optical Technology on Paper, Microform and Magnetic Disk and Tape Storage.* In 1987 almost 89 percent of information storage was on paper. Other methods of storage are magnetic, microform, and optical. Within these nonpaper-based forms of information storage, optical storage on CDROM disks grew from less than seven percent of the market in 1987 to over 32 percent of the market in 1991. During this time period, magnetic storage decreased about 21 percent and microform storage by over four percent.

International Business Machines computers are widely used by banking, insurance, and transportation companies. Their computers also make up a large share of the installed computers being used in government offices, manufacturing plants, and businesses throughout the United States. The optical storage technology they select will have a strong impact on how optical storage of information is adopted by offices all over the country. Customers are seeking greater standardization of CDs. Five-and-one-quarter-inch, 12-inch, and three-and-one-half-inch disks are standard sizes.

As we progress toward the 21st century, education also is undergoing change. Lifelong learning by all age groups, without restrictions on time or place, seems more and more a necessity. Laser disk technology used to store and accumulate knowledge will play an important role in the process. People who have access to the most recent and complete information will have an advantage over those who do not.

Laser disk technology makes it possible to assemble a multitude of current facts and data from many resources. Unlike earlier technological innovations that were mainly labor saving devices, new information technology is viewed as an extension of the thinking power of the human brain. The new technologies not only provide vast information resources and nearly infinite ways to combine them, they can process and transmit that digitized information virtually at the speed of light. Policymakers in government, business, and education can base major decisions on a more comprehensive knowledge than has ever before been available to them.

10 LASERS IN INDUSTRY

(Coherent, Inc.)

A laser machine tool at work

Lasers are powerful tools that have many applications in industry. Lasers are used to cut, perforate, weld, engrave, and heat-treat a great variety of materials. These range from soft rubber to brittle ceramics and even the hardest known substance, diamond. The concentration of intense power and precision of a laser beam make many tasks far more efficient and cheaper to perform than by any other method.

Lightening the Work Load

The need to drill holes is commonplace in industry. Holes in an item as soft as a baby bottle nipple are drilled with laser light. Many items need holes punched through them to enable the user to mount them with screws or nails. In addition, holes are routinely needed in leather and paper goods. Lasers can perforate holes that are smooth, perfectly round, and free of debris or burrs.

With unrivaled speed, pulses from a ruby laser can cut holes of precise gauge through diamonds. These holes are used as dies for drawing metal into wire. The process used to be very time-consuming because it required frequent replacment of high-speed drill tips as well as delays to allow equipment to cool.

Boring holes in heavy metals used to be accomplished with carbide drills or drills with diamond tips. Again, the procedure took many hours and often was interrupted to cool the machinery and replace the drill bits. A powerful laser beam can accomplish the job without friction. Often the hole is completed so quickly that heat from the laser beam is not conducted far from the site of the work and does not affect the rest of the metal.

Laser beams are used to punch holes through plastic, such as the nozzle openings for aerosol sprays. Laser beams also are used to drill fine holes in the edges of contact lenses to allow fluids to flow freely over the surface of the eye. Besides drilling fine holes, lasers detail the thin decals that are used to decorate cars and trucks.

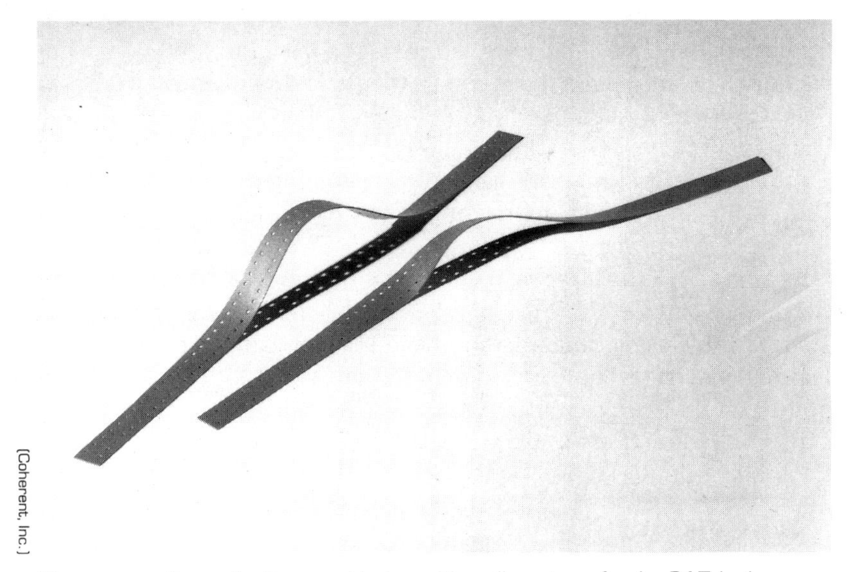

(Coherent, Inc.)

These smooth, perfectly round holes with a diameter of only .017 inch (.43 mm) were perforated in silicone insulator strips by a carbon dioxide laser. This type of material is very difficult to punch mechanically.

Laser light can be used to cut fabric in the manufacture of custom clothing. In his book *The Third Wave,* Alvin Toffler describes how lasers are so efficient at the cutting process that it may be economically possible to cut items of clothing one at a time. Current mass production methods cut up to 500 identically sized garments at a time.

In the future, a shopper could send his or her measurements to the manufacturer over fiber optic telephone lines. The data could be fed directly into a computer that controls a laser cutting machine and a custom-cut garment could be made. In this way, much of the waste of standard-sized clothing would be eliminated. (Just think of all the clothing that is hanging on store racks waiting for the right size person to show up to buy it!) In addition, the heat of the laser sears the cut edges of synthetic fabrics like nylon so they do not fray.

Welding or joining two metals together, whether the smallest wires or huge steel plates, is another application of laser energy. Welds made with lasers are stronger than conventional arc welds, in part because the laser beams are so precise that less of the metal is distorted by the heat of the process. Precision welding is important in many industrial manufacturing processes, such as welding the gears to the synchronizing mechanism in the transmission of an automobile.

The Ford Motor Company uses a laser system to weld the underbody of its automobiles. The laser system achieves a continuous weld that has much greater strength than conventional spot-welding techniques would have. The weld is made at a speed of 500 inches per minute (21 centimeters per second). It only takes one minute to weld together four large panels to form an underbody for an automobile using the laser system.

Industrial carbon dioxide gas lasers producing up to 1,500 watts of power can cut through any material. Moving at high speed, the beam of laser light can engrave patterns, numbers, or letters on metals as tough as steel. If the laser beam moves more slowly, it cuts deeper into the metals. Unlike cuts through metal made with abrasive saw blades, cuts made by laser beam are smoother and more distortion-free. Often, laser cuts made through optical materials are so smooth that they need no further polishing.

Another industrial application of lasers is *surface alloying.* Surface alloying is a material processing method that joins together a surface material with another interior material when treated with a laser beam. Unlike a mere coating of one material over the surface of another material, the two materials melt under the intense heat of the pulsed laser beam and meld together forming an *alloy* at the surface of the material.

(Ford Motor Company)

Automated aligning and welding of trucks at Ford Motor Company

Surface alloying is useful for incorporating corrosion resistance on materials where the resistance is needed only at the surface. Surface alloys can increase the heat and wear resistance of materials that will be used in high-stress conditions. In something as ordinary as a saw blade, surface alloying can strengthen the teeth of the blade without having to treat the whole blade. In some applications, the materials needed to give the desired properties to a metal are rare or very expensive. In these cases, surface alloying can conserve precious resources and be very cost-effective for the manufacturer.

Heat treating metals to harden them is important in the manufacture of automobiles, airplanes, and ships. The metal housing of power steering units for General Motors vehicles are treated with lasers that cost millions. The lasers can be computer controlled to operate automatically. Gears and surfaces that line the cyclinders of automobile engines are heat-treated because they are subject to stress from heat and from repeated contact with other surfaces.

Lasers are particularly good at heat-treating metal items such as automobile parts because their brief but intense heat affects only the selected area. The laser-treated metal undergoes far less distortion and its strength is maintained. Lasers are also used to engrave patterns in heat-treated metal surfaces that trap dirt and thus prevent damage to the raised metal surface.

Making Miniaturization Possible

Laser welding has helped make possible the miniaturization and reliability of many electronic components. Laser beams finer than a human hair can weld together wires as small as four-thousandths of an inch. Lead wires can be attached precisely to electronic components that are smaller than a pinhead. And microchips small enough to be carried by an ant can be connected using laser beams to accomplish the welds in a fraction of a second.

In the manufacture of semiconductors, diodes, transistors, and integrated circuits, controlled amounts of impurities or dopants are introduced near the surface of silicon, the chief material used to make these electronic components. The silicon then needs to be heat-treated or annealed to electrically activate the added impurities.

Lasers are ideal for annealing these components because their precision selectively heats only the very thin layer of impurity-treated regions. Laser annealing helps to make possible miniaturized elec-

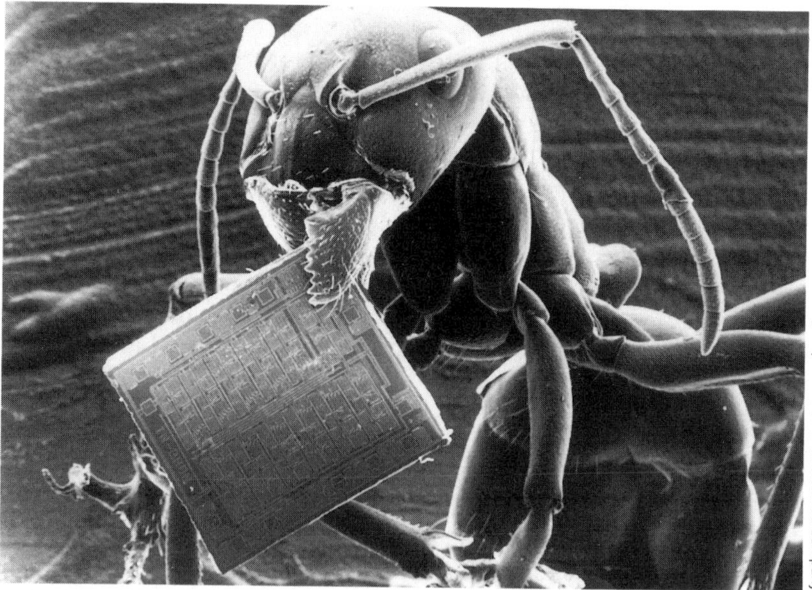

(Philips Consumer Electronics Company)

This electron micrograph of an ant carrying a microchip illustrates the miniaturization of electronic circuitry.

(International Business Machines Corporation)

An IBM–designed laser scanning system automatically verifies circuit patterns on ceramic sheets used in IBM's large-computer chip carriers.

(International Business Machines Corporation)

Pen nib and micro-chip

tronic components such as tiny semiconductor devices the size of a grain of salt.

In the manufacture of microchips, many chips are imprinted onto one slice of silicon or wafer. Because of the minuteness of the circuitry on each microchip, the wafers must be perfectly flat. Lasers are used to analyze the flatness of wafers to within a few thousandths of an inch. In addition, dust-busting lasers are being developed to remove submicroscopic specks that clog stencils used to print circuits that are less than half a micron in width onto wafers.

11 MORE USES FOR LASERS

Today, lasers are being used in seemingly countless ways to improve the quality or efficiency of many everyday tasks. Lasers are also being utilized to do things that were previously impossible to imagine.

Measuring Distances and Motion

Lasers are used to measure accurately distances from the submicroscopically small to the enormously large. For example, the laser beam produced by a helium-neon gas laser is capable of measuring a change in position as miniscule as 10 millionths of an inch. An experiment conducted by the National Bureau of Standards determined that the world's standard meter bar actually was 1.00000098 meters long.

Accurate measurement of extremely small distances can be accomplished using a device known as an *interferometer.* In this device, a beam-splitting mirror divides a laser beam into two parts. One part of the beam is reflected from an immobile or fixed mirror assembly to a photodetector. The second part of the beam is reflected from another mirror assembly mounted on the nonstationary object. The second part of the laser beam rejoins the first part before reaching the photodetector.

If no movement occurs, the two parts of the split laser beam arrive at the photodetector in phase (the crests of the waves of one part of the laser beam match up exactly with the crests of the waves of the second part of the laser beam) and there is no change in light intensity. However, if there has been some movement of the nonstationary object, the split laser beams arrive at the photodetector out of phase. The photodetector records a changing pattern of intensity, alternating between light and dark. By comparing the changes in intensity to the wavelength of the laser beam, an interferometer can measure extremely small movements.

Very large distances can also be measured accurately with laser beams. The astronauts of the *Apollo 11* (1969) and *Apollo 14* (1971) missions left behind permanent light reflecting devices on the moon's surface. Each device consisted of rows of precision optical mirrors set at different angles to receive light from an Earth station and reflect it back.

Pencil-thin pulses from an argon gas laser aimed through a telescope at the the moon traveled through 250,000 miles of space to the moon and only spread to cover a circle about two miles in diameter. Unlike ordinary light, which would have spread out too much to be useful, the laser pulses were still strong enough to be reflected back to Earth.

Scientists measured the time it took for the laser beam to return and then, using the known speed of light, 186,000 miles per second (300,000 meters per second), calculated the distance to the moon accurately to within four inches.

Satellites that reflect laser beams back to Earth can also detect movements of the continents. When the huge slabs of the Earth's crust

Laser range finder used to beam laser pulses to the moon through a telescope to a reflector placed on the moon by Apollo 11 *astronauts*

(Hughes Aircraft Company)

called *tectonic plates* slowly collide, islands may appear, volcanoes erupt, or sections of the Earth quake. Lasers have been used to measure movement of the Earth's crust along the San Andreas fault in California. This major earthquake zone is at the juncture of the Pacific and North American plates. This region also is home to over eight percent of the nation's population and a center for some of the country's critical high technology. For these reasons, scientists have been watching this fault carefully in hopes of being able to predict any major earthquake that may occur.

NASA's LAGEOS (Laser Geodynamics Satellite) was the first dedicated satellite designed solely to measure movements of the Earth's crust using a laser beam. It was launched May 4, 1976, from Cape Canaveral by a Delta rocket. Its surface contains 426 reflectors that can return laser beams striking it from Earth.

In orbit over the Earth, LAGEOS's reflectors return laser beams to three ground stations located on either side of the San Andreas fault. Measurements taken over the course of months or years keep track of the distance and direction in which the Pacific and North American plates are shifting. This important information may help to predict future earthquakes.

Lasers have revolutionized modern-day surveying and mapping. For example, laser surveying was recently used by Dr. Bradford

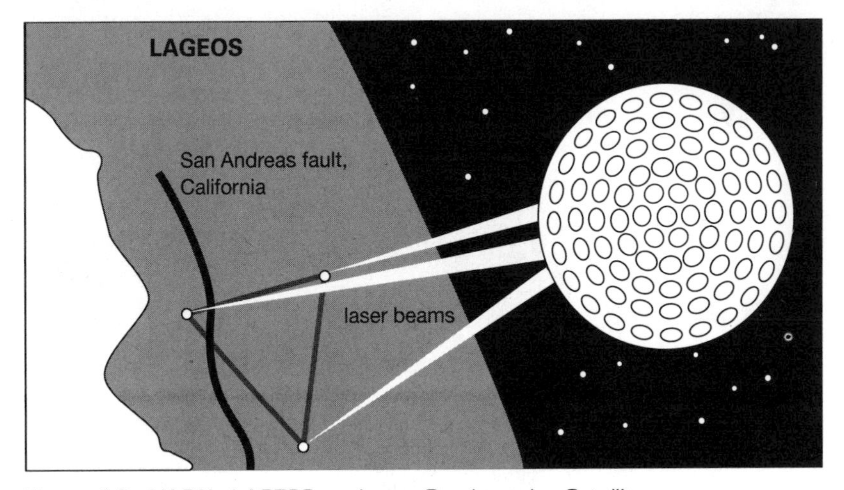

Figure 12: *NASA's LAGEOS, or Laser Geodynamics Satellite, measures the distance and direction in which the Pacific and North American tectonic plates are shifting. The satellite's reflectors return laser beams from three ground stations located on either side of the San Andreas fault to keep track of any changes that may predict a future earthquake.*

Washburn and coworkers to more accurately map the entire Presidential Range in the White Mountain National Forest of New Hampshire. Mirrors placed at strategic points in the mountains reflected laser beams to a range finder that automatically calculated the distance to those points.

The *laser gyroscope* is another technological advance using lasers. Gyroscopes measure angular motion and are used to detect and measure rotation, such as the pitch or roll of ships and airplanes during navigation. Boeing 757 and 767 aircraft and military systems are examples of places where they are used.

In a laser gyroscope, three laser tubes are arranged in a triangle. Two laser beams travel in opposite directions (clockwise and counterclockwise) around and around the triangular path of the laser tubes, which are equipped with mirrors at each corner of the triangle. At one corner of the triangle, a portion of each laser beam passes through the reflecting mirror onto a detector screen. If there has been no motion, the two beams form a known interference pattern on the screen. However, if the gyroscope has been rotated even a tiny amount, the interference pattern on the screen undergoes detectable changes.

Laser gyroscopes are small and lightweight compared to older conventional gyroscopes that used rotating wheels. They also are more reliable and accurate because they have no moving mechanical parts and are frictionless. Laser gyroscopes are so sensitive that they can measure variations in the speed of light caused by the rotation of the Earth.

The military uses lasers in range finders. LIDAR (*li*ght *d*etection *a*nd *r*anging) is similar to RADAR (*ra*dio *d*etection *a*nd *r*anging), except that RADAR uses pulses of microwaves while LIDAR uses pulses of laser light. LIDAR determines the distance to an object by measuring

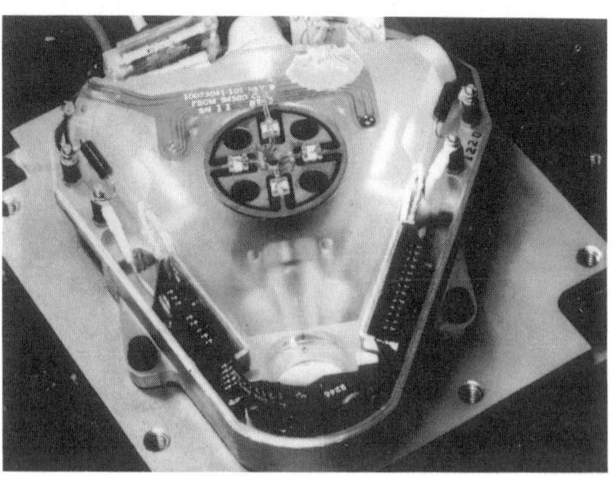

A triangular ring laser gyroscope

(Honeywell, Inc.)

the round-trip time it takes for a pulse of laser light to travel to and from the object. Since the speed of light is a known constant, the distance to the object can be calculated.

The military uses LIDAR to determine how far away enemy targets are. Many modern range-finding devices are compact and portable enough to be brought directly onto the battlefield. An infrared laser emits an invisible beam that is reflected from the target. The range finder has a built-in infrared detector. A microchip computer inside the device automatically calculates the distance to the target based upon the time it takes for the infrared beam to return to the range finder. The laser beam is so narrow that it cannot be jammed unless something is placed directly in its path. An infrared laser beam is invisible to the enemy during the daytime and can also be used after dark.

In military ground action, tanks and other vehicles use ruby- and Nd:YAG laser range finders. The M1 tank uses a forward-looking infrared (FLIR) night-vision system and laser range finder to find enemy tanks and destroy them before they know they are detected or have a chance to return fire. FLIR systems can also be used for

(Hughes Aircraft Company)

A transmitter for a mini-laser range finder being adjusted on U.S. Army attack helicopter

navigation, surveillance and security, detection, and aircraft landing applications.

In 1991, during Operation Desert Storm in the Middle East, television newscasts showed pictures of laser-guided weapons (LGWs) zeroing in on targets and even entering doors of buildings and air shafts of bunkers with extraordinary accuracy. Smart bombs and guided missiles direct themselves to their targets by using a *target designator.* An infrared laser beam is aimed at a target and sticks with it. A bomb or missile equipped with a detector locks onto the infrared laser beam marking the target and then follows the beam to its destination.

LIDAR is also used as an earthwatch technique. For example, LIDAR is used to study clouds of dust and other pollutants from industrial sources or volcanoes. Pulses of laser light are scattered and reflected by particles or clouds in the upper atmosphere. Light returning to the LIDAR is studied to determine the location and how much pollution is present in the air. Some dye-sodium laser systems can scan as high as 50 miles above the surface of the Earth.

U.S. Air Force Forward Air Controllers demonstrate a Laser Target Designator (LTD), which enables them to pinpoint targets for laser-guided weapons.

(Hughes Aircraft Company)

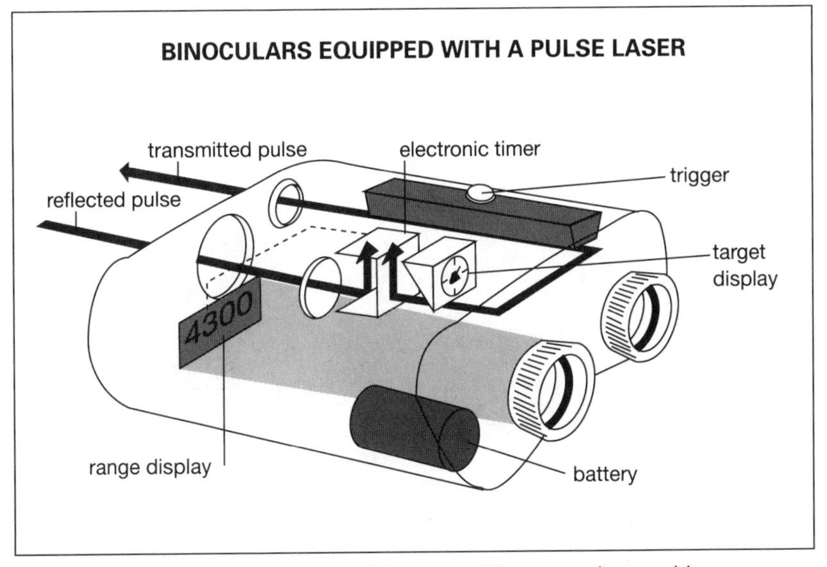

Figure 13: Binoculars equipped with a pulsed laser can be used by a soldier to measure the distance to a target. The soldier sights the target and shoots an invisible pulse of laser radiation toward it. The time taken for the pulse to be reflected back to the range finder is measured, electronically converted into the distance, and displayed for the soldier to read.

At the Max Planck Institute for Quantum Optics in Germany, an excimer-based LIDAR system has been placed on a ship to research the ozone levels in the upper atmosphere in the Arctic and Antarctic oceans.

Lasers and Law Enforcement

Lasers have found several uses in law enforcement. One is to detect speeders. Laser guns that can accurately detect and measure the speed of individual vehicles are being used by police to snare speeders. Using a gun sight, a police officer can aim the laser gun's narrow, invisible laser beam directly at a specific suspected speeding vehicle. Every three milliseconds, the laser gun calculates how far away the car is. It then calculates the speed of the automobile by dividing the change in distance by the elapsed time between the readings.

In addition, lasers can be used to detect fingerprints that previously would have gone unnoticed because they were on print-proof mate-

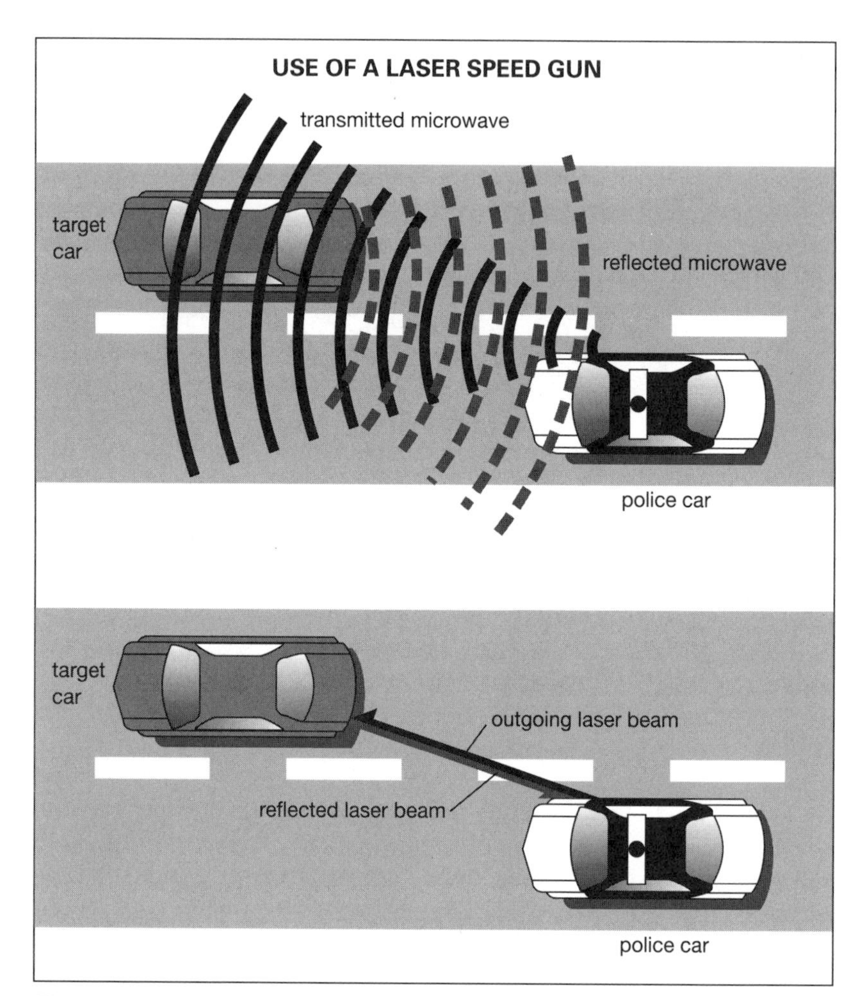

Figure 14: *Police use a speed gun to determine how fast a vehicle is moving. The speed gun emits a beam of microwaves that are reflected back from a moving car to the gun. The targeted car's speed can be measured by comparing the frequency of the outgoing beam to that of the incoming beam. One problem is that the microwave beam may spread out to be 200 feet wide at a distance of 2,000 feet. This can lead to some question about which car in a group actually is speeding. However, if a laser speed gun is used to detect speeders, the beam only spreads to a 5½ foot spot over a range of 2,000 feet. For this reason, a laser speed gun can more accurately target a specific car. Every few milliseconds a laser speed gun calculates the distance to a speeding car by determining how long the laser beam takes to travel the round trip. The speed of the targeted car is equal to the change in distance divided by the time that has elapsed between readings.*

rials such as leather, oily weapons, or human skin. For example, a laser system can make incriminating fingerprints on a Styrofoam cup fluoresce and then display them on a television screen.

Lasers in Construction and Agriculture

Lasers guide construction or agricultural equipment used to level or grade soil. A laser positioned at a construction site sends out a 360° rotating beam that is a constant reference at every point on the site. A receiver mounted on earth-moving equipment, such as a bulldozer, detects the laser beam and uses it as a guide. A control box receives constant grade information that either controls the earth-moving equipment automatically or displays a signal to the operator that the

(Spectra-Physics, Construction and Agriculture Division)

The "One Man Leveling Crew" is used at a construction site. The Laserplane transmitter emits a continuous self-leveled reference plane over a job site area of one acre.

level is high, low, or on grade. In automatic operation, the detector on the earth-mover stays locked on to the laser beam guideline.

In addition to accurate earth moving, laser beams can be used to perfectly align pipes being laid for drainage, water, or sewage systems. Tunnels also can be aligned to vary less than a millimeter in each 100 feet excavated. A laser set up at the end of the tunnel emits a beam that establishes the path to be followed. The excavating machine can have a receiver mounted on it with a display that shows the operator whether the digging is proceeding in the exact desired direction.

Ceilings and walls of buildings can be built perfectly straight with a laser level that uses an established visible laser beam as a reference point. Unlike conventional string plumb lines, laser beams do not sag due to the the Earth's gravity or require constant on-site checking. They are always a perfectly level and straight reference once they are properly positioned on the site.

In agriculture, lasers can guide even relatively unskilled workers to properly contour land for planting or to prepare it for irrigation of major food crops. One manufacturer's laser system is used in many developing countries where grain production is a vital major resource. The laser system cuts the soil preparation time of large land areas to less than half that needed with conventional methods.

Laser Printers

Laser printers use low-power lasers to form the images of letters of the alphabet and other characters on a rotating drum. Dry, inklike powder adheres to the images formed on the drum, then is transferred to paper to print the desired text.

Laser printers are much quieter than other printers and can print over 13,000 lines per minute or 10,000 sheets of letter-size paper in an hour. The quality of the type is far superior to dot matrix printers and looks more like an individually typed letter quality type.

Uniform Product Code

Many products now have a *Uniform Product Code* (UPC) symbol printed on their packaging. The UPC symbol consists of a series of dark lines of various thicknesses printed against a light background. It represents an identifying number assigned to the product by the Uniform Product Council, Inc. The purpose of these printed lines is to allow merchants to use laser scanners instead of conventional

(International Business Machines Corporation)

A laser scanner is used to scan the UPC code on a package of sugar at a supermarket.

keying of a cash register to tally products when they are purchased. Laser scanners are used in modern supermarkets and large chains of stores because they are more accurate and faster than humans.

A laser beam scans or "reads" the UPC bar code on each product as it is passed over a window in the scanner. The information is received by a detector and passed on to a computer. The computer instantaneously signals the cash register to print the name of the product and its price. At the same time, the computer uses the UPC information to inventory the items being purchased so that store owners know when to reorder stock. All of the necessary information is automatically recorded.

Shedding New Light on Old Art and History

Lasers are being used to restore old art treasures. In a 1971 visit to Venice, Italy, a San Diego physicist, Dr. John Asmus, found that he could restore and preserve valuable works of art with a laser. An accumulation of layers of dirt on marble sculptures that were exposed to salty air, pollution, flooding, and disrespectful birds could be burned off with a laser beam without harming the art piece itself.

Dr. Asmus has since cleaned and restored paintings, including Indian rock paintings that were vandalized in Utah in 1979, 14th-century frescos in Italy, murals in California, as well as buildings and monuments.

Another way in which lasers are helping to restore the past is through the realistic reconstruction of historical figures. In the city of York in northern England, a restoration project depicts life in a Norse village in the year 948. Among the displays is a figure named Eymund. Eymund was reconstructed from a Viking skeleton found in an archaeological dig at Fishergate.

Eymund's skull was mounted on a turntable and scanned with a low-power laser. As his skull rotated, the reflected laser beam was recorded by a video camera that was connected to a powerful computer. The computer stored all of the information about the shape and size of the skull.

The next step in the reconstruction process was to laser scan a living man of the same age and build as Eymund. Again, the computer recorded all of the data. The computer combined the two sets of data and molded the living person's face around the Viking skull.

(York Archaeological Trust)

Eymund with sculptor and skull used to recreate his facial features

Next, a milling machine controlled by the computer shaped hard foam into a three-dimensional head. In addition, photographs produced by the computer were used by a sculptor to add lifelike expression and color to Eymund's face.

In this way, Eymund was reconstructed to produce a display so realistic, that Dr. Dominic Tweedle, chief of archaeology with York Archaeologic Trust's Jorvik Center said, "When I first saw him I was stunned by his naturalness. I'm sure that if one of Eymund's Viking contemporaries were alive today, he would recognize him."

Researchers have learned that the skull and facial muscles determine the shape of a person's face. They have found out that a laser scan reconstruction looks like the historical person, not the modern-day person. Proof of this has come from forensic medicine. The reconstructed faces of murder victims have been recognized by their relatives when skulls have been restored using this technique.

Of Laser Light Shows and Fairies

Laser light shows, a seemingly magical mix of music and light, have become popular in many major cities in the United States and other countries. The first one was produced in 1973 in Los Angeles and the idea spread from there. Even some discotheques have switched to laser lights and no longer use strobe lights for effect.

The brilliantly colored images seen in a laser light show usually are produced using argon lasers or krypton lasers. Prisms, scanners, mirrors, and other optical devices diffuse and reflect the laser light to form fantastic shapes, clouds, and patterns of color on a backdrop of a dark nighttime sky or planetarium dome. A laserist who creates and controls the light images choreographs the vibrant moving light to suit the beat and theme of the music.

In addition to laser light shows, lasers have been used to create special effects in theaters for live stage shows. A production of *Peter Pan* on Broadway used a computer-controlled argon laser beam to play the role of Tinkerbell. The translucent laser light beam flitted around the stage as though it were a true fairy.

12 LASERS: SEARCHLIGHT FOR SCIENTIFIC RESEARCH

This photo shows laser excitation beams as they pass through the flow chamber of a multi-laser flow cytometer that is used to sort and analyze cells in biological research.

(Los Alamos National Laboratory)

Lasers are used extensively in many areas of scientific research. Lasers are powerful tools used to investigate the structure of atoms and molecules as well as the very nature of chemical reactions. In biological studies, laser light in the visible range interacts with organic materials such as the pigments chlorophyll (the green color in plants), hemoglobin (the red color of blood), and melanin (the brown color in skin). Ultraviolet laser light is absorbed by proteins and the nucleic acids of the cell.

Chemical and Biological Research

Laser spectroscopy is a technique used to investigate reactions in biological processes as well as changes in the structure of molecules. One kind of laser spectroscopy known as *flash photolysis* can probe fleeting chemical reactions that are measured in nanoseconds (billionths of a second) or picoseconds (trillionths of a second). Lasers are capable of producing intense light pulses of very brief duration to study these reactions at subatomic speeds as never before possible.

Examples of processes being studied with this technique are photosynthesis (the manufacture of food by green plants) and vision. In addition, the excited states of molecules of *deoxyribonucleic acid* (DNA) and molecules involved in reactions in the *mitochondria* of the cell have been studied. DNA is the material that makes up the genes people inherit from their parents. The mitochondria sometimes are nicknamed the powerhouses of the cell because they are the site of energy production. They are found outside the nucleus in cells.

Another kind of spectroscopy known as *Raman spectroscopy* has been revitalized and revolutionized by lasers. In 1928, Indian physicist C. V. Raman noted that light passing through the molecules in a solution was altered in wavelength. Information about the structure of the molecules could be deduced from observing the changes in the wavelength.

The availability of intense laser light has greatly increased the sensitivity and high-resolution of information that can be learned about molecules using Raman spectroscopy. Tunable lasers have even made possible probing the very vibrations within molecules.

With lasers as sources of finely focused monochromatic wavelengths of light, even more can be learned about the structure of molecules. Dr. Arthur Schawlow of Stanford University wrote in an article in *Science* magazine that the "purity" of light emitted by lasers "makes possible unprecedented resolution of fine detail. With lasers, we are finding possibilities and many new ways to probe deeply the nature of matter."

Cell function can be studied by altering specific parts of a cell in the laboratory. A laser can be focused through a microscope onto miniscule parts of cells such as the mitochondria or the chromosomes. The technique is called *microirradiation.*

In cells that do not contain pigments, selective dyes are used to stain the cell parts. A microbeam from a laser then can delete, for example, tiny regions on chromosomes. From these fine-tuned genetic studies, researchers can learn the function of the genes on a specific region of a chromosome.

Isotope Separation and Fission

Another way in which lasers are being used is to trigger chemical reactions. In addition to understanding the structure of atoms and molecules, researchers want to be able to boost the rate at which some reactions occur. An important application is *isotope separation.*

Atoms have set numbers of protons and electrons in them. However, some atoms of the same element may have differing numbers of neutrons in their nucleus. For example, ordinary carbon atoms have six protons, six neutrons, and six electrons, whereas carbon-14 atoms have eight neutrons in the nucleus. Carbon-14 is an *isotope* of the carbon atom. An isotope has the same number of protons but a different number of neutrons than is normal for that element. Because carbon-14 is radioactive, it can be used to date the age of fossils and the rocks in which they are found.

The radioactive element uranium, U-238, is far more abundant than its isotope, U-235. The isotope, U-235, can fuel *fission,* the chain reaction needed to generate atomic power or the explosion of an atomic bomb. U-238, however, actually inhibits the process. Conventional methods of separating the two forms of uranium are very expensive and only garner about half of the U-235 available.

Lasers can be used to preferentially dissociate molecules of a particular isotope. In January 1990, the secretary of energy submitted the Department of Energy's *Plan for the Demonstration, Transition, and Deployment of Uranium-AVLIS Technology* to the U.S. Congress. The plan is a program that will lead to construction of a uranium atomic vapor laser isotope separation (U-AVLIS) plant for uranium enrichment. If successful, this would effectively increase the supply of U-235 as a nuclear energy resource and keep the United States competitive in the international uranium market as a supplier to utilities.

The Lawrence Livermore National Laboratory and two industrial partners, Martin Marietta Energy Systems, Inc. and Westinghouse Idaho Nuclear Company, are working together to develop AVLIS technology for use commercially.

The two types of lasers used for AVLIS are high-power copper-vapor lasers and dye lasers. Applications include the more efficient purification of materials used to manufacture semiconductors and X-ray sources that would allow the manufacture of direct random-access memory (DRAM) microchips with storage capabilities that may have a memory capacity measured in gigabits (Gbit). (A giga is a billion.)

Fusion: Recipe for a Star!

An important application of lasers is in *nuclear fusion.* The sun is a natural source of radiant energy that results from the process of fusion.

Under the tremendous pressures and at the 20 million degree temperatures found on the sun, hydrogen atoms fuse or join together to form helium. During the fusion process, enormous amounts of energy are released. As a comparison, the amount of energy released from fusion is about a million times greater than from a chemical reaction such as the burning of fossil fuels.

At the Lawrence Livermore National Laboratory experiments are being conducted in *inertial confinement fusion,* or ICF. In these experiments, the process of fusion is replicated on a miniature scale in the Nova, the world's most powerful laser. Repetition of the process could produce a continuous supply of energy for electric power generation.

In the Nova ICF reaction, a small, hollow capsule is filled with a mixture of two isotopes of hydrogen known as deuterium and tritium. Bursts of laser light are focused on the surface of the capsule, intensely heating it in a few billionths of a second. The outer shell of the capsule vaporizes producing conditions that simulate the birth of a star. The deuterium and tritium are compressed and heated to fusion conditions during the ICF process.

(Lawrence Livermore National Laboratory)

Target chamber of Nova, the world's most powerful laser

ICF researchers at the Lawrence Livermore National Laboratory have a recipe for a "laser-produced 'star' for use in a full-scale electric power plant. Fill a five-millimeter-diameter capsule with five milligrams deuterium-tritium fuel. Apply 300 trillion watts of power and wait 10 billionths of second. Result: one miniature star!"

The amount of energy produced in a fusion reaction is awesome. The energy from one ounce of fuel in a fusion reactor could provide enough power for four people and their household for up to 50 years. It is estimated that 300 tons of coal would need to be burned to yield the same amount of energy. Many of the fuels humans have depended upon for energy are shrinking in supply. Also many of them are of environmental concern; for example, the burning of fossil fuels such as coal produces air pollution problems. Energy derived from nuclear fission in today's power-generating plants results in leftover radioactive waste.

In contrast, the Earth has an abundant supply of fusion fuel that could supply enough energy for the entire population of the planet for millions of years. The primary fuel for the fusion reaction is deuterium which is available in ordinary seawater. It is estimated that the oceans contain 40 billion tons of deuterium. Tritium is produced

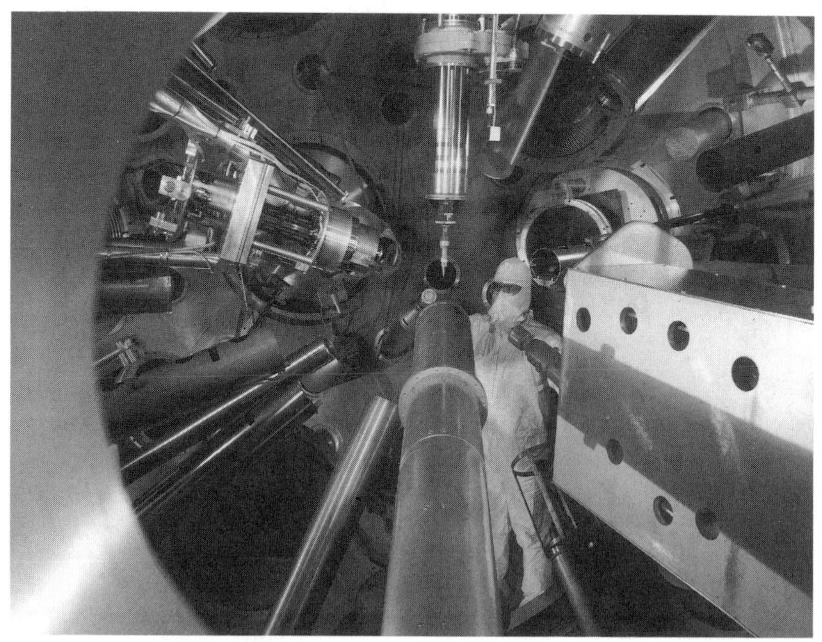
(Lawrence Livermore National Laboratory)

Inside of the target chamber of Nova

(Lawrence Livermore National Laboratory)

This pin-point-sized star was created when researchers fired the Nova laser at a tiny fuel capsule.

from lithium, a common metallic element. The fusion process does not produce radioactive waste. Fusion energy would be inexhaustible, clean, and safe.

Laser Launches, Lightcraft, and Star Wars

The Strategic Defense Initiative Organization has funded the development of laser systems to put microspacecraft into orbit with a direct launch system known as a rail gun. Much of such a system still must be developed and tested, but the technology would require lasers that could deliver 20 to 50 megawatts of power for the 10 to 20 minutes it takes to put a payload into orbit. The payloads are called "microspacecraft" because they are very small, weighing under 50 pounds.

A prototype futuristic way to fly into space or to travel anywhere in the world within 45 minutes is already on the drawing boards. Students and faculty members at Rensselaer Polytechnic Institute

(RPI) are studying a laser-propelled spacecraft called a Lightcraft. It would literally ride a laser beam into orbit.

A small Lightcraft Technology Demonstrator (LTD) is being researched and worked on now at RPI for possible launch by the late 1990s. The 264-pound, single-stage orbit vehicle will use a 100 megawatt ground-based free electron laser to transmit power directly to the spacecraft's engine. Powerful laser pulses focused on the spacecraft will heat air and fuel to propel the vehicle into space like a laser-heated pulsejet.

The LTD may make possible an affordable family spaceship sometime in the next century. A Lightcraft reduces the cost of space transportation and travel by 1,000 times when compared to the space shuttle. The technology to build the LTD exists today. The successful demonstration of the LTD could lead the way to the building of larger Lightcraft capable of carrying up to five people into space.

Research on the Strategic Defense Initiative, also dubbed Star Wars, is being pursued as a future defense system by the United States. Constellations of powerful lasers positioned in space could blast enemy satellites or intercontinental nuclear missiles launched at the United States by an aggressor before they would be able to reach their targets.

(NASA)

Artist's conception of solar pumped laser in space

13 HOLOGRAPHY

Lasers make possible a fascinating form of photography known as *holography. Holos* means "complete" and *graphos* means "picture" in the Greek language. A hologram records a complete, three-dimensional picture of an object. When observed, a hologram looks so convincing that the viewer has the uncanny sensation of being able to reach out and touch the real object.

In comparison, photographs are recorded images of the intensity of ordinary, incoherent light. They are two-dimensional because it is difficult to systematically measure the random phases of incoherent light. A hologram, on the other hand, is made with coherent laser light. Coherent light waves that are out of phase can be measured to produce a three-dimensional record of the depth of every detail of an image.

A New Dimension in Photography

In 1947, Professor Dennis Gabor, a researcher at London's College of Science and Technology, discovered the principle of holography while seeking ways to increase the resolution of fine detail in pictures of objects seen with electron microscopes. He described his work as "an experiment in serendipity."

Gabor passed the light from a mercury-vapor lamp first through a pinhole and then through a green filter, to produce a spreading beam of nearly coherent green light. The beam could be recorded on a photographic film or plate.

Next, Gabor placed a film in front of the beam of green light and the object he wanted to photograph behind the film. The green light first striking the film had a regular wave pattern. However, the light reflected back from the object behind the film had an irregular wave pattern that was a complete record of the irregular shape of the object. The two sets of waves met at the surface of the film, producing an

Dennis Gabor

(American Institute of Physics, Niels Bohr Library, Weber Collection)

interference pattern on the film. This method produces a *reflection* hologram.

To recreate the image recorded on the film, Gabor directed green light from the original source through the film. A person viewing the backlit film could see the three-dimensional image of the object. In addition, the image changed as the viewer moved to another position, just as if the real object were being seen.

Gabor's discovery was significant, but the light sources available at the time were neither bright enough nor pure enough to produce strong, clear images. Only when lasers became available could his idea begin to be used in practical ways.

In the early 1960s, Emmett Leith and Juris Upatnieks produced the first laser holograms at the University of Michigan. They were able to use the bright, coherent light of laser beams and devised another improvement to Gabor's work as well. Instead of aiming all of the laser light through the film, they aimed the beam onto a beam-splitting mirror. Part of the beam traveled directly to the object before being reflected back to the film. The second part of the beam was reflected

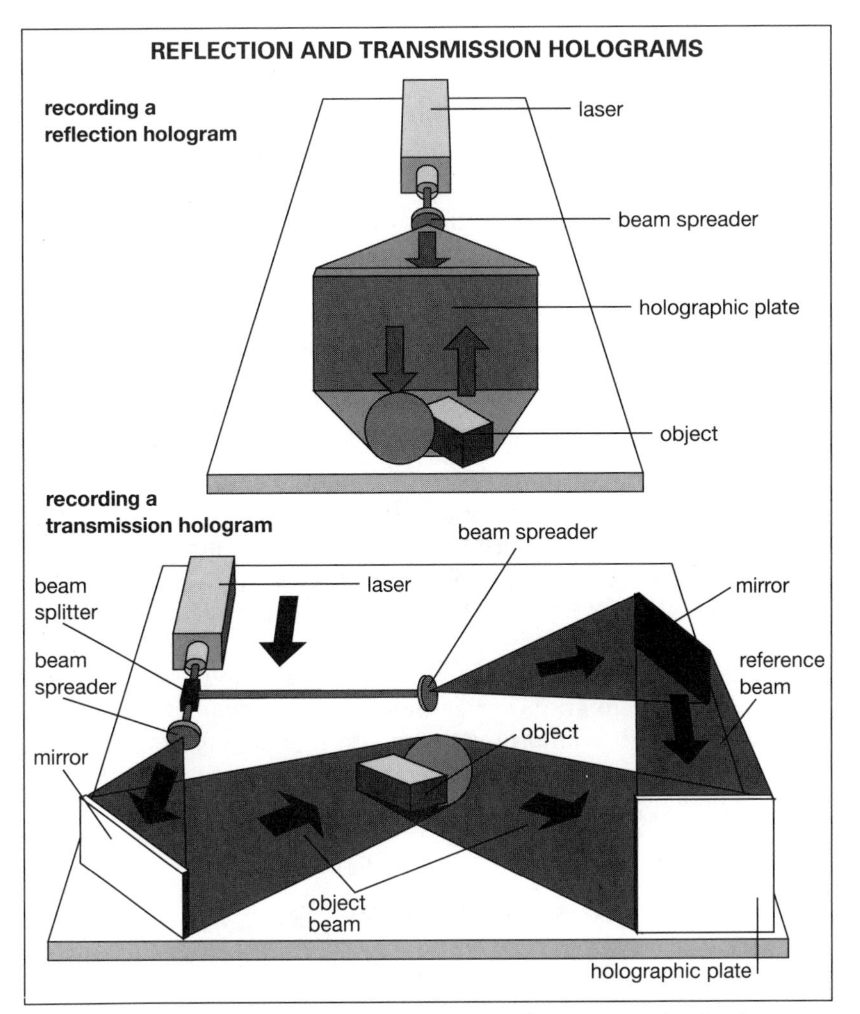

***Figure 15:** Holograms can be recorded in two different ways. A* reflection *hologram is made by directing a laser beam through a holographic plate to an object behind the plate. The laser beam first striking the plate has a regular wave pattern. The laser beam reflected back from the object to the plate has an irregular wave pattern. A* transmission *hologram is made by splitting a single laser beam into two parts. The* reference beam *is reflected from a mirror directly to the holographic plate without bouncing off the object. It has a regular wave pattern. The* object beam *travels to the object before being reflected to the holographic plate. It has an irregular wave pattern. In either kind of hologram, the interaction of the regular wave pattern with the irregular wave pattern on the holographic plate creates an interference pattern that is a complete record of the information needed to recreate a three-dimensional image of the object.*

from another mirror back to the film without having bounced off the object.

A hologram produced using Leith and Upatnieks's method is a *transmission* hologram. The *reference beam* travels directly from the output laser to the *holographic film.* The second laser beam, the *object beam,* is reflected off all of the surfaces and parts of the object. When the object beam arrives at the holographic plate, it has a range of phase delays, which are recorded on the plate as an *interference pattern.*

Recall that an interference pattern is a record of light and dark lines. Light lines occur where the light waves are in phase (the crests of the waves exactly match each other). Dark lines occur where the light waves are *not* in phase (the crests of the waves are out of step with each other).

To view the holographic image of the object, a laser beam is directed onto the interference pattern on the holographic film. The interference pattern delays the waves in the laser beam to reconstruct the three-dimensional image of the object. Whereas a two-dimensional photograph looks the same from all angles, a three-dimensional hologram looks different when it is seen from various vantage points, just as the real object does.

Because the wavelength of light is so small, holograms must be made in stable, vibration-free settings. Even movement of less than half a wavelength would blur the resulting holographic image. For this reason, special tables and equipment are used to produce clear, bright holographic images.

Applications of Holography

There are many applications of holography. In industry a hologram can be made of a perfect model of an item that is to be manufactured, such as a ship's propeller. When production gets under way, a hologram of each newly manufactured propeller is superimposed on the hologram of the defect-free model. Defects show up as variations from the perfect model because they produce an interference pattern. This process of finding flaws is called *holographic interferometry.*

Holographic interferometry is the most sensitive tool industry has ever had. It can be used to pinpoint changes due to vibration or heat. It even can detect the change in form of a concrete slab made by the weight of a dime!

By combining computer graphics with holographic techniques, three-dimensional holograms of architectural or engineering projects can be generated. This gives the architect or engineer a first-hand preview of what a building will look like inside and out. It can also be used to correct unforeseen problems before building actually is started.

With the advent of X-ray holography, scientists for the first time can record three-dimensional views of live (wet), intact cells and the micropscopic structure within the cells. Only X-ray lasers are sufficiently bright to make a hologram within the micro timescale of about 50 picoseconds, short enough to freeze the motion in a living, active sample cell.

In 1968 Dr. Stephen A. Benton invented transmission holograms that could be viewed with ordinary light. This made possible the mass production of holograms. Utilizing an embossing technique, the interference pattern of holograms can be stamped into plastic and reproduced millions of times for a cost of only pennies per piece.

Because quality holograms cannot be counterfeited easily, holograms now appear as logos on credit cards as a means of maintaining security. In 1982 losses due to forgery of credit cards jumped to $11,000,000 from $740,000 the previous year. This prompted Visa to add a representation of its trademark dove-in-flight hologram to its credit cards. In addition, the credit card numbers cannot be modified without altering the hologram.

Military applications of holography include *pattern recognition*. Missiles carry a stored memory bank of holograms of hundreds of different views of enemy targets, such as tanks or airplanes. After launch, the missile illuminates possible targets with laser light. It then compares the information with the holograms of enemy targets in its memory bank. The missile is capable of automatically seeking, recognizing, and ultimately destroying enemy targets without further guidance from the launch area.

Airplane pilots, both civilian and military, now have devices called head-up displays that assist them in landing, especially in foul weather conditions that limit their vision of the runway. These instruments produce holographic displays of flight-path data on a see-through screen right before the pilot's eyes. With the convenient, transparent display, the pilot can see information gathered from a variety of instruments in the cockpit and the runway at the same time and can concentrate more fully on a safe and uneventful landing.

Holography holds great promise for storage of the vast quantities of information that have become available in the age of information and computers. Holograms reduce information to the dimensions of the wavelength of light used to store it. Up to 30 million bits of computer information can be stored on a four-by-six-inch microfiche using holography.

With holography, data also can be stored in layers on the different planes of a solid crystal. In this way, the entire volume of the crystal can be used for storage. Theoretically, all of the information available in the Library of Congress could be stored on a holographic medium about the size of a sugar cube!

In the November 10, 1990 issue of *New Scientist,* an article reports that researchers at the Swiss Federal Institute of Technology in Zurich are trying to increase the quantity of information that can be stored by recording many holograms on top of each other on a single polymer film. Using different frequencies of light from a tunable dye laser, the scientists were able to record multiple images on the same film. The technique may make possible 100,000 times greater storage capacity than on today's hard computer disks.

Another advantage to storing information as holograms is that all areas of a hologram record information about an object. For this reason, damage to one portion of a hologram will not completely

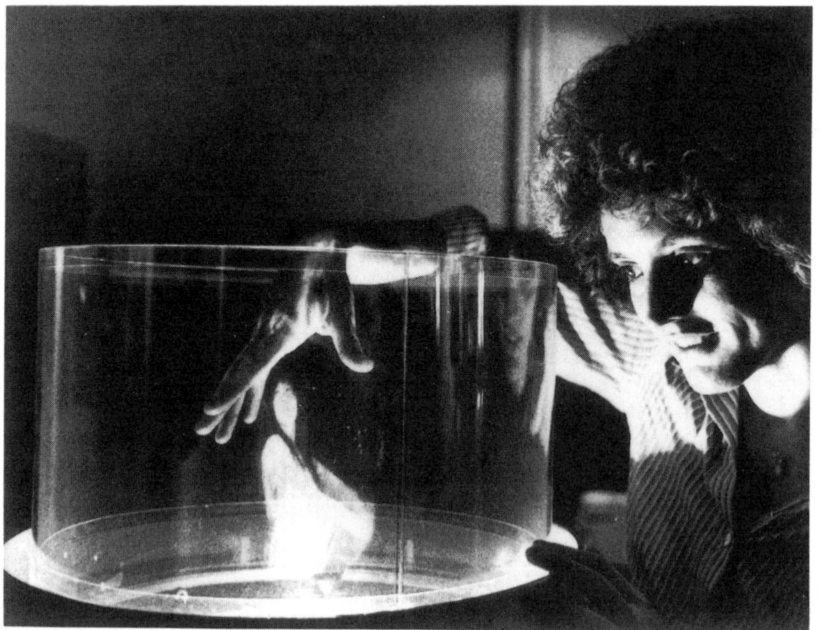

(Museum of Holography)

Rosemary Jackson Smith, the founder of the Museum of Holography in New York City, reaches into holographic stereogram by Peter Claudius.

destroy the information. Scratches or dust on a hologram therefore do not pose as serious a problem as they do with ordinary photographs.

Some scientists are studying how the human brain stores information. They have found that the human mind seems to mimic a hologram. It stores information, not in one precise point or isolated neuron, but spread over a region of the brain. Patients who have had a portion of their brain injured, for example, still can remember pieces of information, though perhaps not with the same efficiency.

Holographic Art

Artists have used holography to create new art forms. Some have produced holograms on glass plates that look like sculptures floating in air. When the viewer moves, the perspective and even the color of the art image changes as well.

Not all three-dimensional holographic images are still forms. An image of a moving dancer at the Museum of Holography in New York City is an example of an *integral* hologram. Some artists are concentrating their efforts in the production of integral motion holograms.

14 SAFETY WITH LASERS

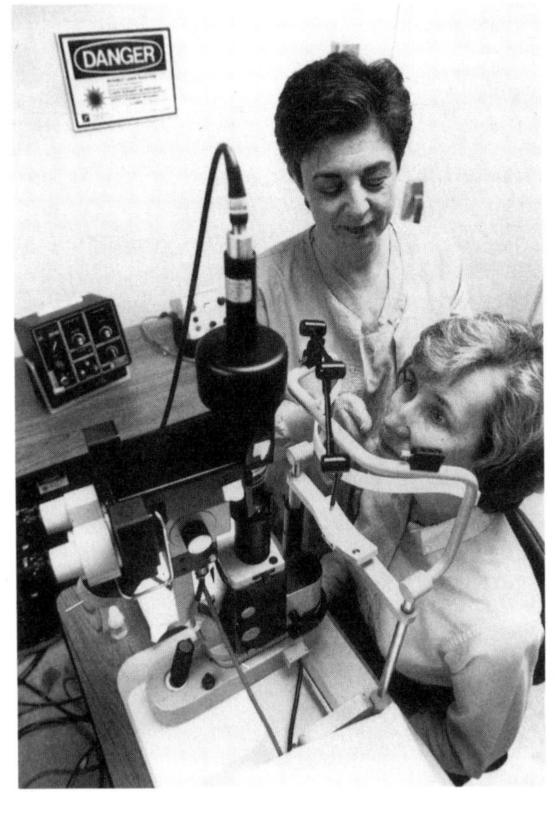

A patient being readied for laser eye surgery. DANGER sign is prominently displayed to warn people to take proper precautions to prevent damage to their eyes.

(U.S. Food and Drug Administration)

Lasers are capable of producing extremely powerful beams that could be dangerous to people who work with them. A system of classifying lasers according to the hazard they present was produced between 1965 and 1972.

In the United States, the classification of lasers follows standards published by the American National Standards Institute (ANSI) and by the Bureau of Radiological Health (BRH) of the U.S. Food and Drug Administration. The standards set by these two sources are very similar.

Class I, or Exempt, lasers produce no known hazard to workers. The lasers in supermarket checkout scanners and in video disk players are in this group. Even if people looked at a Class I laser for several hours, they would not injure their eyes. Therefore, no safety rules are necessary for users of Class I lasers.

The next group, Class II, or Low Risk, lasers, would cause damage to people's eyes if they looked directly into the laser beam for a long time. Examples of Class II lasers are the helium-neon lasers often used in classroom demonstrations. These lasers have a yellow "CAUTION" sign that directs users not to stare directly at the beam.

The Class III, or Moderate Risk, lasers can produce a beam powerful enough to damage the retina of the eye. This would result in pinpoint blind spots in the eye. Lasers in this group can cause retinal damage faster than a person can blink to avoid exposure. These lasers have a red and white "DANGER" sign to warn people not to allow the beam directly to enter the eye.

The fourth group of lasers, Class IV, or High Risk, can cause serious eye damage even from scattered reflections of the original beam. In addition, the beam can cause serious burns on the skin if it is exposed to the energy of the beam.

(Hughes Aircraft Company)

A Hughes Aircraft Company laser technician wears protective eyeglasses as he observes a ruby laser piercing a hole through a sheet of extremely hard tantalum metal.

Class IV lasers are usually used in research laboratories and in restricted workplaces where the users are carefully controlled. These lasers are enclosed with a cabinet that protects operators from exposure to the laser beam when the laser is in operation. In addition, a protective device prevents the laser from being operated when the protective cover is removed.

Class IV lasers have a "DANGER" label that includes information about the wavelength, laser medium, pulse duration, and maximum output of laser radiation.

Though the best laser hazard control is to completely enclose the High Risk laser system, this is not always possible. Commercial protective goggles usually are designed to prevent particular wavelengths from reaching the eye and should be marked to indicate the range of wavelengths for which they are effective. Users of Class IV, High Risk, lasers *must* wear eye protection.

CONCLUSION

Lasers have already proven their potential. When they were first available, some skeptics said lasers were, "a solution in search of a problem." But in the light of the present, we clearly can see their worth. From delicate eye surgery that can save a person's sight, to heavy-duty welding of industrial machines, to the fastest way to communicate, to the purest light for scientific research, lasers have become one of the most important and revolutionary tools of our time.

In the future, many more uses will be found for lasers. In the Spring/Summer 1979 issue of *Stanford Magazine,* Dr. Arthur Schawlow talked about the potential of lasers:

> *As lasers have been improved, they have found an enormous range of important applications. As we learn more about how to make them and apply their subtle powers, they will inevitably find many more places in technology, and even in the arts.*
>
> *In ways that science fiction never dared imagine, lasers may serve us in the future. . . . Entirely new and radically different kinds of lasers will probably appear, and as our knowledge of light and matter grows, lasers will make practical what can barely be done today, and make possible what we have not yet even dreamed of.*

APPENDIX OF PREFIXES

Prefixes indicating very small units:

Milli-	One thousandth	0.001
Micro-	One millionth	0.000001
Nano-	One billionth	0.000000001
Pico-	One trillionth	0.000000000001
Femto-	One quadrillionth	0.000000000000001

Prefixes indicating very large units:

Mega-	One million	1,000,000
Giga-	One billion	1,000,000,000

GLOSSARY

Active medium The material in a laser which, when excited by an outside energy source such as electricity, amplifies light in a laser.

Amplification The process by which light is intensified in a laser.

Atom The smallest particle of an element that can exist and still be that element. Atoms are made up of smaller subatomic particles such as electrons, protons, and neutrons.

Binary code A representation of numbers, letters, or even sound waves as two signals or digits. In the case of pulsed laser light, zero represents when the light pulse is OFF and one represents when the light pulse is ON.

Bit In a binary code, each zero or one is a *bi*nary digi*t*, or *bit*.

Byte A group of eight bits.

Coherent light Light waves emitted by a laser are described as coherent because they are in phase with each other, all of the same wavelength, and all traveling in the same direction.

Conductor A material that easily allows electricity to pass through it, such as copper, aluminum, gold, or other metals.

Decoder A device that converts the pulses of laser light in a fiber optic telephone line back into electrical waves.

Detector-repeater A device in a fiber optic telephone line that strengthens or amplifies the laser light beam before it passes through the next segment of the optical fiber.

Deuterium The isotope of hydrogen that has one neutron and one proton in its nucleus and, therefore, has twice the mass of ordinary hydrogen. It is found in seawater and sometimes is called heavy hydrogen.

Digitized The process by which laser pulses are converted into a binary code of only two signals, zero or OFF and one or ON.

Directional Laser light travels in straight beams that do not spread out as much as ordinary light.

Doping The process of adding an impurity to a pure crystal to give it a desired property. For example, chromium oxide is the doping material, or impurity, used in a ruby laser crystal that consists of aluminum oxide.

Electromagnetic spectrum The range of radiant energy that is all around us and that consists of radio waves, microwaves, infrared rays, visible light, ultraviolet light, X rays, and gamma rays.

Electron The subatomic particle that moves in an orbit around the nucleus of an atom. Electrons are negatively charged.

Encoder A device that measures the waves of electricity in a fiber optic telephone system and converts them into a series of eight ON-OFF pulses of laser light.

Energy source The source of energy that is used to excite the active medium of a laser. Energy sources may be a strong ordinary light, electricity, a chemical reaction, or another laser.

Excited state lifetime The brief period of time when an atom is in an excited, unstable state.

Feedback mechanism Two mirrors or other reflective surfaces that are at each end of the active medium in a laser. The mirrors build up the strength of the laser beam by bouncing photons back and forth through the active medium.

Fission The splitting of an atomic nucleus that results in the release of enormous amounts of energy.

Frequency The number of waves that pass a given point within a specific unit of time.

Fusion The joining together of hydrogen atoms to produce helium. During the process of fusion, enormous amounts of energy are released. Sometimes fusion is called a thermonuclear reaction because extremely high temperature is needed for fusion to occur. Fusion is the process by which the sun produces radiant energy.

Ground state The condition of an atom or molecule when all of its electrons are at their lowest energy level.

Hertz A unit used to measure electromagnetic wave frequency; equal to one cycle per second.

Holography The process of making or using a hologram. A hologram is a three-dimensional picture made without a camera on a photograhic film or plate. The hologram itself consists of an interference pattern of light and dark lines that, when illuminated by a beam of coherent light, produces a three-dimensional picture of an object.

Host material A pure material used to manufacture a laser or semiconductor. In the ruby laser crystal, aluminum oxide is the host material and chromium oxide is the doping material, or impurity.

In phase Light waves that are in step with each other are in phase; the crest of each wave is matched with the crests of all the other waves.

Incoherent light Light waves that are a mixture of many different wave lengths traveling in different directions.

Insulator A material that does not allow electricity to pass through it such as plastic, glass, or rubber.

Interference pattern A pattern of light and dark lines produced when light waves are not in phase with each other. The light portion of the pattern is where the crests of light waves overlap or are in phase and the dark portion of the pattern is where the crests of light waves do not overlap and are not in phase with each other.

Ion An ion is an atom (or group of atoms) that has a positive charge or a negative charge. A positively charged ion is an atom that has lost one or more of its electrons. A negatively charged ion is an atom that has gained one or more electrons.

Isotope An atom of an element that has a different number of neutrons in its nucleus than usual. Carbon-14 is an isotope of the ordinary carbon atom because it has eight neutrons in its nucleus instead of the usual number six.

Laser *L*ight *a*mplification by *s*timulated *e*mission of *r*adiation.

LIDAR *Li*ght *d*etecting *a*nd *r*anging. LIDAR is similar to RADAR (*ra*dio *d*etecting *a*nd *r*anging, which uses pulses of microwaves) except that LIDAR measures the time it takes for a pulse of laser light to travel to and from an object to determine the distance to the object.

Maser *M*icrowave *a*mplification by *s*timulated *e*mission of *r*adiation. Masers are similar to lasers except that they emit microwaves, which have much longer wavelengths than laser beams.

Mode-locking A technique that uses a dye solution as a shutter to produce very short, powerful pulses of laser light spaced at regular intervals.

Molecule The smallest particle of a substance that has all of the properties of that substance and that is made up of one or more atoms.

Monochromatic Ideally, monochromatic light is all of one color or wavelength. When monochromatic light passes through a prism, it emerges as a single, straight beam of the same color that entered.

N-type A material doped with negatively charged atoms. N-type material is used to manufacture semiconductor lasers.

Neutron A subatomic particle that has no charge. Neutrons are found in the nuclei of atoms (except for the element hydrogen, which consists of only one proton and one electron).

Nucleus The positively charged central part of an atom. The nucleus of an atom consists of one or more protons and one or more neutrons (except for the element hydrogen, which has only one proton in its nucleus).

Optical fiber An optical fiber is a hair-thin, flexible thread of ultra clear glass through which laser light can pass without losing its brightness. Optical fibers also are known as lightguides.

Outer coupler The partially reflective mirror in a laser feedback mechanism that allows the laser beam to escape.

P-type A material doped with positively charged atoms. P-type material is used to manufacture semiconductor lasers.

Photon The basic unit of electromagnetic radiation also known as a quantum.

Pockels cell A special switch used as a very fast shutter inside a continous wave laser to produce brief, enormous pulses of laser light.

Population inversion A necessary condition for laser action to occur. It exists when there are more excited, high-energy atoms present in the active medium of a laser than low-energy atoms.

Proton A positively charged subatomic particle found in the nucleus of an atom.

Quantum The basic unit of electromagnetic radiation also known as a photon.

RADAR *Ra*dio *d*etecting *a*nd *r*anging. RADAR uses pulses of microwaves to determine the distance to an object by measuring the time it takes for microwaves to travel to and from the object.

Random access memory (RAM) Permits access to stored data in any order or sequence that the user desires.

Read only memory (ROM) Stored data that only can be read by the user.

Reflection hologram A hologram made by passing a laser beam through a holographic film or plate placed in front of the object that is to be pictured. Laser light reflected from the object back to the film records the irregular shape of the object as an interference pattern on the film.

Semiconductor A substance that is neither a good insulator nor a good conductor of electricity. Its properties can be altered with doping materials so that it can serve as either an insulator or a conductor. Silicon, which is found in ordinary sand, is commonly used as a semiconductor material.

Solitions Special electromagnetic waves that do not alter their shape, even when traveling over long distances. Solitions may make possible the transmission of laser pulses through long lengths of optical fibers such as transoceanic telephone cables, without the need to install expensive regeneration equipment to strengthen the pulses of laser light.

Spontaneous emission Excess energy released by an atom or molecule as it returns from an excited state to a lower energy level or the ground state. The energy is emitted as a photon of radiant energy.

Stimulated emission Energy released (in the form of photons) as the excited atoms or molecules in a population inversion return to a lower energy level or ground state. These photons, in turn, cause other excited like atoms or molecules to emit additional identical photons.

Transmission hologram A hologram made using a laser beam that has been split into a reference beam and an object beam. The reference beam is reflected by a mirror and then travels directly to the holographic film or plate. The object beam travels to the object, is reflected off all of the surfaces and parts of the object, and then travels to the holographic film or plate where it produces an interference pattern. The picture recorded in a transmission hologram is viewed by directing a laser beam onto the holographic film or plate.

Tritium An isotope of hydrogen that has two neutrons and one proton in its nucleus and, therefore, has three times the mass of ordinary hydrogen. It is produced from lithium, a common metallic element.

Velocity The speed with which something moves. Velocity is measured in units of distance per unit of time, such as miles per hour. The speed of light is 186,000 miles per second or 300,000 kilometers per second.

Volt The unit of electrical potential difference and electromotive force. It is used to measure the electrical potential difference between two points of a conductor. Electromotive force is that which causes a flow of electric current.

Watt The unit of electric power or rate of work. One watt is approximately 1/746 of a horsepower; one horsepower is 746 watts.

Wavelength The distance between successive waves as measured from the crest of one wave to the crest of the next wave.

FURTHER READING

Books

Bender, Lionel. *Lasers in Action.* East Sussex, England: Wayland Publishers Limited, 1985. This 48-page book is a good introduction to lasers. It is illustrated with many informative color photographs and drawings.

DeVere, Charles. *Lasers.* New York: Gloucester Press, 1984. This book for young readers is clearly written and abundantly illustrated with drawings that show many applications of lasers.

Filson, Brent. *Exploring with Lasers.* New York: Julian Messner, 1984. This 96-page book discusses lasers and their many uses. It is illustrated with black-and-white photographs and line drawings.

Johnson, James. *Lasers.* Milwaukee, Wisconsin: Raintree Publishers Inc., 1981. This book is for young readers who want an introduction to the subject of lasers. It is illustrated in color.

Kettlekamp, Larry. *Lasers: The Miracle of Light.* New York: William Morrow and Company, 1979. This informative 128-page book is written for readers older than those of the other children's books on this list. It is well illustrated with black-and-white photographs and line drawings.

Maurer, Allan. *Lasers: Lightwave of the Future.* New York: Arco Publishing, Inc., 1982. This 174-page adult book has more detailed information about lasers than the other books on this list. It is illustrated with black-and-white photographs.

McKie, Robin. *Lasers, The Electronic Revolution.* New York: Franklin Watts, 1983. A good introductory book about lasers for young readers. This book is illustrated with many helpful drawings and photographs.

Taylor, J. R., and French, P. M. W. *How Lasers Are Made.* New York: Facts On File, 1987. This oversized 32-page book covers the basics about lasers. It is filled with color photographs, illustrations, and charts that greatly enhance the text.

Articles

Boraiko, Allen A. "The Laser, A Splendid Light for Man's Use," *National Geographic*, March, 1984, pp. 335–377. This is a beautifully illustrated article that is very readable and that captures the excitement of laser technology.

Maurer, Allan. "Torch of a Thousand Suns," *Modern Maturity*, April-May, 1988, pp. 56–61. An easy-to-read introductory article.

INDEX

Italic numbers indicate illustrations.

A

active medium 3, 19–20, 22, 107
Air Force, United States 30
alloy 70–71
American Academy of Ophthalmology 44
American National Standards Institute (ANSI) 102
American Optical 20
American Physical Society 14
American Telephone and Telegraph 39
amplification 4, 107
Apollo 11 *76*
Apollo 14 76
argon laser *13*, 24–25, 30, *32*, 45, 47, *55*, 87
Army, United States 44
arthoscope 53
Asmus, John 85–86
astigmatism 47, 50
atherosclerosis 56
atom 4–5, *5*, 6–7, *7*, 18, 89–90, 107

B

balloon angioplasty 56
Basov, Nikolai 15, *22*
Bell, Alexander Graham *29*, 30, 35
Bell Laboratories 15, 31–33, 39
Bell Telephone Company 39
Bell Telephone Research Group 21
Bennett, Jr., William *31*, 32–33
Benton, Stephen A. 99
binary code 37, *38*, 61, 107
binary digit 37, 62
bit 39, 62, 100, 107
bit rate 37
Bohr, Niels 7
boule 20
Bressler, Neil M. 46
Bressler, Susan B. 46
Brotherton, Manfred 31–32
Bureau of Radiological Health (BRH) 102
byte 39, 107

C

Cape Canaveral 81
carbon dioxide gas laser 4, 22–23, 50–53
carbon-14 90
cataracts 44, *46*
CDROM disk 56–66
chemical laser 23
chlorophyll 88
chromium oxide 20
chromosome 89
classification of lasers, 103–104
Claudius, Peter *100*
clean room 37
coherent light *12*, 95, 107
Columbia Radiation Laboratory 15
Columbia University 14, 16
compact disk (CD) 3, 61, *64*, 64–66
compact video disk (CDV) 3, 61, *64*, 64–65
conductor 28, 107
Congress, United States 94
continuous wave (CW) laser 2, *24*, *26*, *27* *62*
copper vapor laser 90
cornea *46*, 47, *49*, 49–50
crucible 20

D

data transmission 3, 30, 36–40, 66–67
decoder *37*, 107
dental laser 64
deoxyribonucleic acid (DNA) 89
detector-repeater 39, 107
deuterium 91–92, 107
diabetic retinopathy 47, *48*
digitized 37, 61, 107
directional light 12, 107
direct laser revascularization 57
direct random-access memory (DRAM) microchips 90
Disney World 39
doping 20, 72, 108

E

Einstein, Albert 8, *9*, 15
electrodes 21, 26
electromagnetic spectrum 9, *10*, 11, 108
electromagnetic waves 8
electron *4*, *5*, 6–8, 21, 90, 108
Electronic Trend Publications 66
electrosurgery 58
encoder *37*, 108
endometriosis 52, *53*
energy level *5*, 5–7, *7*
energy source 3, 4, 108
EPCOT (Experimental Prototype Community of Tommorow) Center 39
error correction code 62
excimer laser 25, 49, 56
excited state lifetime 7, 108
Explorer XXXVI *13*, 30
Eymund *86*, 87

F

farsightedness 47, *49*, 49–50
feedback mechanism *3*, 108
fiber optic cable (TAT-1, TAT-7, TAT-8) 39
fission 89–90, 108
flashtube 1, 18
Food and Drug Administration, United States, (FDA) 49, 52, 57, 60, 102
Ford Motor Company 70, *71*
forward-looking infrared (FLIR) night-vision 79
frequency 10–11, 108
fusion 90–92, 108

G

Gabor, Dennis 95, *96*
gall bladder 3, 62
gallium aluminum arsenide (GaAlAs) laser 27
gamma rays *10*, 10–11
gas laser 5, 21, 23, 31–33
General Motors 71
genes 89
Geusic, J. E. 20
glaucoma 44, 46
Goddard Space Flight Center *13*, 30
Gordon, James P. *14*, 15
Gorley, Paul *26*
Gould, Gordon 16–17
ground state 7, 30, 108

H

Halstad, A. Stevens *24*, *32*
helium-neon 5, 22
helium-neon laser 4, 21–22, *31*, 32–33
hematroporphyrin derivative (HpD) 56
hemoglobin 88
Herriott, Donald *31*, 32–33
Hertz 11, 32, 108
HI-OVIS 40
hologram 95, *97*, 98–99
holographic art *100*
holographic film or plate *97*, 98
holographic interferometry 98
horsepower 21
host material 20, 109
Hughes Aircraft Company 1, *103*
Hughes Research Laboratories 18

I

Illinois, University of 15
impurity 20, 72
incoherent light *12*, 109
industrial uses of lasers
  cutting fabric 74
  drilling holes 73

heat treating metals 2, 68, 71, 76
miniaturization 77
surface alloying 75
welding 3, 68, 70–72, *71*
inertial confinement fusion (ICF) 91–92
infrared rays 9, *10*, 11, 26, 83, 84
in-phase light 12, 98, 109
insulator 26, 109
integral hologram *100*, 101
interference pattern 8, 78, *97*, 98, 109
interferometer 75–76, 80
International Business Machines (IBM) 20, 26, 66
interpolation 63
ion 24, 109
ion laser 24, *24*
iosotope 90, 91, 109
isotope separation 89–90

J

Javan, Ali *22*, *31*, 33
Johns Hopkins University 50
Johns Hopkins University School of Medicine 46, 50
Johnson, L. F. 20
Journal of the American Medical Association 47, 49

K

Kennedy Space Center 41
krypton 25
krypton laser 24, 46–47, *55*, 87

L

LAGEOS 77, *77*
Lankard, J. R. 26
laser, acronym 2, 17
laser, kinds of. *See specific kinds.*
laser, parts of *3*
laser action 3, 4, 8, 17
laser-guided weapons (LGWs) 80
laser gyroscope *78*
laser light show 89
laser manufacturing 20
laser mapping and surveying 81
"One Man Leveling Crew" *83*
laser printer 3, 84
laser scanner 87
laser spectroscopy 26, 88, 89
laser speed gun 81, *82*
laser subgingival curettage 58
laser surgery 43–56, *45*, *52*, *55*, *102*. *See also specific kinds of surgery.*
Laser Target Designator (LTD) 80
Lawrence Livermore National Laboratory 90–92
Lebedev Physics Institute 15
Leith, Emmett 96
lens, of eye *46*, 47, *49*
LIDAR (light detection and ranging) 78–81, 109
Lightcraft Technology Demonstrator (LTD) 93–94
light-emitting diode (LED) 27
lightguide 34
lithium 96
liquid dye laser 25
London's College of Science and Technology 95
Louisiana State University (LSU) Eye Center 49–50

M

macula 44, *46*, 47
macular degeneration 44–46, 48
Maiman, Theodore *1*, 17, *18*, 19
Marcos, H. M. 20
Martin Marietta Energy Systems, Inc. 90
Maryland, University of 15
maser *14*, 14–16, 109
Max Planck Institute for Quantum Optics 81
Maxwell, James Clerk 8
McCarthy, Delwin 59
McDonald, Marguerite 50
melanin 88
meter bar, standard 75
Michigan, University of 96
microchip 36, *72*, *73*, 74
microirradiation 89
microspacecraft 93
microwaves 9, *10*, 11, 14–16, *82*
mitochondria 89
mode-locking 28, 109

Modified Chemical Vapor Deposition (MCVD) 35
molecule 15, 109
Mollenauer, Linn F. 40
monochromatic *12*, 109
Morse code *38*
Museum of Holography *100*, 101
Myers, Terry 58

N

Nassau, K. 20
National Aeronautics and Space Administration (NASA) 30, 77
National Bureau of Standards 75
National Eye Institute 47
Navy, United States 14
nearsightedness 47, *49*, 49–50
neodymium:yttrium aluminum garnet (Nd:YAG) laser 20, 44, 53–54, 58, 79
neutron 6, 90, 110
New Scientist 100
Nobel prize 15
North American Air Defense Command 41
Northwestern University 59
Nova *91*, *92*
n-type 27, 110
nuclear fusion 94
nucleus 6, 110

O

object beam *97*, 98
ocular histoplasmosis 46
Operation Desert Storm 80
optical fiber 3, 30, 34–36, *36* 39, 40–42, *41*, *55*, 55–56, 110
- cladding 35
- core 35, 40
- manufacturing 34–35, *36*

optical maser 16
optic nerve 44
oscillations 9
output coupler *3*, 3–5, 110

P

pattern recognition 99
Peter Pan 87
phased coupled array 27
photocoagulate 45
photodetector *62*, 75
photodynamic therapy (PDT) *55*, 56
photon 4, *5*, 8, 17–18, 21, 29, 30, 110
photophone *29*, 30
photo-refractive keratectomy (PRK) 49
photosynthesis 89
Physical Review 16
Pick, Robert M. 59
pits, CD 61
Pittsburgh, University of 44
Planck, Max 8
planetarium 90
Pockels cell 27, 110
pollutants 84
population inversion 4, 110
posterior capsulotomy 44
preform *34*, 35
prism 12–13, 90
Prokhorov, Aleksander M. 15
proton 6, 90, 110
p-type 27, 110
pulse 2, 22, 29
pump 4, 17–18, 21

Q

quantum 8, 9, 110

R

RADAR 78, 110
radial keratotomy 47
radio 30
radioactive waste 96
radio waves 9, *10*, 11
rail gun 96
Raman, C. V. 92
random access memory (RAM) 90, 110
range finders 76, 78–79, *81*, 109–110
Readers' Guide to Periodical Literature 66
read only memory (ROM) 65–66, 110
reference beam *97*
reflection hologram 96, *97*, 110
Rensselaer Polytechnic Institute (RPI) 93–94
repeater *37*, 40–41
retina 44–45, *49*
retinal detachment and tears 46, 46–47

rhodamine 4, 25
ruby *1*, 3, 4, 17, *18*, 19
ruby laser 5, 69, 79, *103*
Rutherford, Ernest 6

S
San Andreas fault *77*
Sandia National Laboratories *26*
satellite 13, 30–31, 76–77
Schawlow, Arthur 15–17, 89, 105
Science 89
semiconductor 28, 110–111
semiconductor or diode laser 5, 26–27, 36–37, 62, 72, 74
silicon 36, 72
Smith, Rosemary Jackson *100*
Snitzer, Elias 20
solar pumped laser *94*
solitions 39–40, 111
Sorokin, Peter P. 20, 26
sound waves 31
space shuttle 41
speed of light 8, 11, 76
spontaneous emission 8, 111
Stanford Magazine 108
Stanford University 89
Stark, Walter J. 50
Star Wars (Strategic Defense Initiative) 94
Stevenson, M. J. 20
stimulated emission 4–5, *5*, 8, 15–16, 111
Strategic Defense Initiative (SDI) Organization 93–94
Swiss Federal Institute of Technology 100

T
tectonic plates *77*
telephone 29, 37. See also *optical fiber.*
The Third Wave 70
Toffler, Alvin 70
Townes, Charles H. *14*, 14–17
transition-cell carcinoma 53
transmission hologram 97, 98–99, 111
transverse excitation atmospheric (TEA) laser 23
tritium 91–92, 111
tunable dye laser 25, 46, 56, 90
Tweedle, Dominic 87

U
ultraviolet light (UV) *10*, 10–12, 26
Uniform Product Code (UPC) 84–85, *85*
Uniform Product Council, Inc. 84
Upatnieks, Juris 96
uranium atomic vapor laser isotope separation (U-AVLIS) 90
uranium-235, uranium-238 90

V
Van Uitert, L. G. 20
velocity 11, 111
Viking skeleton, laser reconstruction of 86
visible light 9–11, *10*, 16–17
visible spectrum 11–12
Vista-United Telecommunications 39
voltage 24

W
Washburn, Bradford 77–78
Watson Research Center 27
wavelength *10*, 11, *12*, 111
waveguide carbon dioxide laser 23
waves 8–12
Weber, Joseph 15
Westinghouse Idaho Nuclear Company 90

X
X-ray holography 99
X rays *10*, 11

Y
York Archaeologic Trust 87

Z
Zeiger, Herbert 15